# EL SALVADOR STORIES

*Attaining an Education Despite Poverty and Violence*

...............................................

Jerry F. Westermeyer, PhD

El Salvador Stories: Attaining an Education Despite Poverty and Violence
© 2020 Jerry F. Westermeyer, PhD
All rights reserved.

This book or parts thereof may not be reproduced in any form, stored in a retrieval system, or transmitted in any form by any means without prior written permission of the authors, except as provided by United States of America copyright law.

Cover Photo: Neal Erickson
Cover Design: Hyliian Graphics
Interior design: The Author's Mentor
www.theauthorsmentor.com

ISBN: 9798633110760
Also Available in eBook form.

PUBLISHED IN THE UNITED STATES OF AMERICA

For my mentors in social justice actions:

Basil O'Leary, my most influential and wise college teacher and subsequent lifelong friend, and

Brother Denis Murphy, my valued and kind high school teacher, who cofounded Su Casa Catholic Worker and the Br. David Darst Center in Chicago, Illinois.

# Table of Contents

PREFACE .................................................................................. 1
CHAPTER 1   THE GIRL BEGGING AT THE GAS STATION ................. 17
CHAPTER 2   INTERVENTIONS: WHAT WORKS? ............................. 27
CHAPTER 3   DOCTOR SARA .............................................................. 36
CHAPTER 4   THE DISAPPEARANCE OF A DAUGHTER ..................... 43
CHAPTER 5   "PEACE BE WITH YOU" ................................................ 50
CHAPTER 6   THE CHOICE .................................................................. 58
CHAPTER 7   JORGE AND ERIKA: SIBLINGS ...................................... 64
CHAPTER 8   HOPES AND DREAMS ................................................... 74
CHAPTER 9   MORE STUDENT STORIES ............................................ 83
CHAPTER 10  STUDENTS SPEAK ......................................................... 93
CHAPTER 11  LISIA: FROM DROPOUT TO WIFE AND MOTHER ..... 102
CHAPTER 12  HOPE: THE POOR STRUGGLE TO LIVE ...................... 106
CHAPTER 13  "KILL ME HERE": TERROR ON A BUS ........................ 113
CHAPTER 14  MENTAL ILLNESS AND TRAUMA .............................. 118
CHAPTER 15  ALBERTO: ESCAPE FROM GANG LIFE ....................... 129
CHAPTER 16  EMPOWERING WOMEN .............................................. 141
CHAPTER 17  DIALOGUE WITH THE POOR ...................................... 148
CHAPTER 18  SUMMING UP ............................................................... 156
    REQUEST FOR DONATIONS .......................................................... 167
    ACKNOWLEDGEMENTS ................................................................ 169
    REFERENCES .................................................................................. 171
    PHOTO ALBUM .............................................................................. 179

# PREFACE

........................................................

"San Martín, El Salvador—Rosa Ramírez pleaded with her son, urging him not to leave and head north with his wife and young daughter. The risks were simply too high.

"He saw no other choice. Their neighborhood was controlled by a gang that enriched itself through drug-dealing, extortion and violence. But most pressing of all, Ms. Ramírez said, they could barely make ends meet on their jobs at fast-food restaurants and had pinned their hopes on making it to the United States.

"They never did.

"Last Sunday, after weeks on the road, Ms. Ramírez's son, Óscar Alberto Martínez Ramírez, 25, and his 23-month-old daughter, Angie Valera, drowned while trying to cross from Mexico into Texas.

"Their fate, captured in a searing photograph of father and daughter lying face down in the muddy waters of the Rio Grande, her arm limply wrapped around him, has quickly become a focal point in the debate over the stream of migrants pushing toward the American border."

– Kirk Semple, *The New York Times*, June 28, 2019

Although news reports, like the one above, document the harrowing experiences of migrants from Central America seeking asylum in the United States, less well known are the millions of people who may face similar conditions and may be internally displaced yet remain in Central America. This book explores the lives of individuals coping with poverty and the threat of violence while remaining in El Salvador. It presents their efforts to obtain an education and escape the cycle of poverty and a culture of violence spawned by street gangs in the aftermath of civil war. In addition, this book describes a scholarship program designed to help impoverished youth achieve their dreams of education and employment within their own country.

El Salvador is one of the three Northern Triangle Central American countries, which also includes Honduras and Guatemala, from which large numbers of desperate people attempt to flee an epidemic of violence for asylum in the United States (Frazier, 2012; Seeke, 2017; Wolfe, 2017). El Salvador is a small country (roughly the size of Massachusetts) located along the Pacific Ocean and bordering both Honduras and Guatemala. It is the most densely populated country in Central America, with approximately 6.5 million people.

Over most of Salvadoran history, a small oligarchy controlled most of the country's wealth and governing authority and employed security forces to violently suppress popular and broad-based dissent (Wolfe, 2017). These conditions sparked a horrendous civil war from 1980 to 1992, in which about 75,000 people died and many others were left crippled or impoverished (Frazier, 2012). The civil war pitted the Farabundo Martí National Liberation Front (FMLN), a populist, revolutionary force seeking a greater share of wealth and opportunity and supported by Soviet bloc countries, against the

Nationalist Republican Alliance (ARENA), the conservative, established oligarchy of wealthy landowners and military leaders supported by the United States and allied countries (Frazier, 2012; Wolfe, 2017).

El Salvador became a battleground for conflicts involving the major world power blocs during the Cold War. The competing powers poured arms and resources into the small country, and the war continued for a long time and with a more devastating result because of this involvement. El Salvador has a long history of political and economic instability. For decades prior to the civil war, a series of military dictatorships ruled the country (Frazier, 2012; Seeke, 2017; Wolfe 2011, 2017).

The assassination of Archbishop (now Saint) Óscar Romero in March 1980 brought worldwide attention to El Salvador and intensified the civil conflict (Moodie, 2010). Romero, the Catholic religious leader in El Salvador from 1977 to 1980, worked alongside the country's predominantly Catholic residents. Initially, the wealthy, political elites of El Salvador, backing the established government, considered the appointment of Romero by the Vatican in 1977 a safe, conservative choice. Romero was not considered an outspoken liberation theology or social revolutionary leader (Frazier, 2012). However, in the late 1970s, he became increasingly discontented with the failure of the Salvadoran government to investigate murders of priests and others espousing social activism to address injustices. Especially upsetting to Romero was the murder of a close friend, Father Rutilio Grande, in 1977 (Romero, 2018;

Moodie, 2010).

Romero began to oppose the government's lack of response to Grande's murder as well as the social injustices he observed in the country. In radio addresses, Romero increasingly advocated resistance to injustices embodied in government authority. On the day before he died, Romero requested that soldiers put down their arms rather than kill fellow citizens (Moodie, 2010). He was assassinated as he celebrated Mass on March 24, 1980 at the Hospital Divina Providencia Chapel in San Salvador, the nation's capital. More than 12 years later, the Commission for Truth in El Salvador investigated the murder and concluded that right-wing elements in the government planned and carried out the assassination (Moodie, 2010).

Other murders receiving widespread attention during the war years were the rape and murder of three North American Catholic nuns and a religious lay worker in December 1980 by National Guard soldiers (Moodie, 2010); the murder of six Jesuit priests, their housekeeper, and her teenage daughter in 1989; and the killing of hundreds of civilian residents by government soldiers in El Mozote, El Salvador, in 1981 (Frazier, 2012).

The Salvadoran Civil War ended in 1992 with a United Nations-brokered peace treaty between the warring parties (Frazier, 2012; Seeke, 2017; Wolfe, 2017). Its conclusion was facilitated by the end of the Cold War between the United States and the former Soviet Union that sponsored the two warring parties and exacerbated the conflict (Frazier, 2012). The 1992 peace accords led to the establishment of a Truth Commission, whose decisions all sides agreed to accept (Frazier, 2012; Wolfe, 2017).

Although the Truth Commission found that both sides had committed acts of murder and torture against innocent people, most incidents (90% or more) could be attributed to government actions and related right-wing death squads (Frazier, 2012; Wolfe, 2017). To facilitate the peace accords, amnesty was granted in 1993 to all engaged in the conflict (Frazier, 2012).

With the end of the Cold War, the war-weary factions in El Salvador brought to conclusion the peace process that had been under negotiations for years (Frazier, 2012). All parties could agree that the war would continue unabated unless there was a negotiated settlement (Frazier, 2012; Wolfe, 2017). A coalition government established by the peace accords followed with reconciliation efforts between the former enemies as well as land reform to address poverty in the country. As part of the peace accords, new police authorities consisted of elements from right-wing government forces (i.e., ARENA), left-wing revolutionary forces (i.e., FMLN), and other parties.

Following decades of military rule, the first civilian president was elected in the 1980s. In the post-war period, four conservative presidents were followed in 2009 and 2014 by two left-wing presidents (Seeke, 2017). In March 2019, Nayib Bukele was elected president and took office in June 2019. President Bukele headed a new, center-right party that was neither the ARENA nor the FMLN parties.

Rather than be governed by military dictatorship as it has been for most of its history, El Salvador has been governed by popularly elected, civilian, political figures in the post-war period (Seeke, 2017; Wolfe, 2017). Other changes in the post-war period include the transformation of the FMLN into a political party, a more open press, the abolition of the old security force (and its death squads), judicial reforms, and reduced poverty rates (Wolfe, 2017). Most importantly, post-war elections have peacefully transferred presidential and government authority from one leader or political party to another through regular, popular elections.

Unfortunately, a fledgling, developing democracy at the conclusion of a destructive civil war, El Salvador did not escape continued violence or government corruption under some of its elected officials. Two of the last four presidents have been arrested for corruption and a third has fled the country.

El Salvador has had a gang problem since the 1970s that significantly increased following the civil war (Wolfe, 2011, 2017). Initially the gangs occupied marginal territories in comparatively small numbers (Wolfe, 2017). Many of these early gangs dissolved or were absorbed into two primary gangs, Mara Salvatrucha (MS-13) and Calle Dieciocho (18th Street), that began in Los Angeles and then established themselves in El Salvador following the Civil War through US deportation policies (Wolfe, 2017).

Salvadorans escaping the violence of the civil war traveled north to the United States as undocumented refugees. In Los Angeles, they struggled to overcome the trauma of war in El Salvador and the crime and poverty in marginal neighborhoods. In response, some Salvadorans joined existing gangs (such as the 18th Street gang), or started their own (such as the MS-13 gang), to address minority identity issues or to protect themselves from established street gangs and other perceived dangers in urban areas (Frazier, 2012; Wolfe, 2011, 2017).

Large numbers of these undocumented gang members were deported back to Central American countries following the civil war (Wolfe, 2017). Thus, the two most prominent gangs operating in El Salvador today were founded in the United States and have thousands of members in El Salvador, Guatemala, Honduras, the United States, and other countries (Wolfe, 2017).

The gang culture existing in El Salvador since the 1970s radically expanded during the post-civil war period because large numbers of gang members have been deported from the United States back to El Salvador since the civil war. The internal growth of gangs and the deportation of gang members from the United States strained the scarce resources in El Salvador and other Central American countries as gang activity, the murder rate, and extortions dramatically increased in the post-war period (Frazier, 2012; Wolfe, 2017). In recent years, El Salvador, Guatemala, and Honduras recorded some of highest murder rates in the world for countries not at war (Wolfe, 2017).

Gang members control territories within marginal communities in El Salvador and typically identify themselves with tattoos (although this is less common) and mark their territories with graffiti.

Their major source of income is extortion monies (or *renta*) from small- and medium-sized businesses within their territory (Wolfe, 2017). A 1993 survey reports that 43% of the population had already indicated a gang presence in their community (Wolfe, 2017).

The control of street gangs is quite complex. Many factors, including the civil war upheaval and an ingrained culture of violence promulgated across several decades of oppressive military rule, provided a fertile environment for the emergence of violent street gangs in parts of El Salvador (Wolfe, 2011, 2017). Residents of gang-controlled neighborhoods are often extorted and live in fear of gang violence.

Homicide rates fluctuate and exact accuracy is sometimes questionable. Nevertheless, El Salvador historically has had a high homicide rate. In 2009 the homicide rate was about 71 per 100,000 inhabitants, one of the highest murder rates in the world. In 2015 El Salvador's homicide rate reached a post-civil war high of about 103 murders for every 100,000 residents (Wolfe, 2017). By comparison, the United States, itself possessing a comparatively high murder rate, had less than five murders per 100,000 residents that year. Although the homicide rate in El Salvador continues to decline from its 2015 high, it is still one of the highest in the world year after year. The World Health Organization considers a homicide rate over 10 per 100,000 inhabitants to be an epidemic that bears a high economic and social cost (Wolfe, 2017).

Various factors, including street gang violence, contribute to El Salvador's high homicide rate. The two primary gangs and several minor gangs are in violent conflict with one another and with the police/military authorities. Homicides are often committed with impunity. For example, of all the homicides committed in El Salvador in 2005, only 3.8% were investigated by the authorities (Wolfe, 2017).

El Salvador is one of the poorest countries in Central or South America and faces severe economic challenges (Seeke, 2017). A high unemployment rate makes gang involvement more attractive to adolescents and young men without job or education opportunities.

In a recent interview (Bukele, 2019), President Bukele maintains that El Salvador's "whole economy is in shatters." Tourism and business investments have been limited because of the ongoing violence in the country. A 2016 study suggests that about 15% of El Salvador's gross domestic product (GDP) was lost due to violence in the country (Seeke, 2017). President Bukele believes El Salvador should bear responsibility for the steady migration north and address issues of economic duress and insecurity (Semple, 2019b).

An estimated 2 million Salvadorans live in the United States (Wolfe, 2017). Many of them send money (remittances) to relatives in El Salvador, accounting for about 16% of Salvadoran GDP in 2013 alone (Wolfe, 2017). These remittances are vital to the financial well-being of El Salvador and are an important source of income for many people living in poverty.

Although it is difficult to get an accurate number, estimates of gang membership in El Salvador range from 30,000 to 100,000 members for various years (Wolfe, 2017). These gang members extort about 70% of the businesses in the country (Martinez, Lemus, Martinez & Sontag, 2016).

Most gang members are poor, and the majority of their victims are also poor. Most extortions involve small amounts of money. Street gangs thrive in marginal, impoverished communities where the disadvantaged are more likely to be extorted and boys and young men are coerced to join gang activity. Rather than finding large financial rewards, most gang members find a group identity and respect in gang membership. Sometimes they find security in which they feel protected from other predatory gangs (Martinez et al., 2016).

## CURRENT INVOLVEMENT IN EL SALVADOR

....................

My friend, John Kukankos, was a Peace Corps volunteer in El Salvador from 1970 to 1972. I first visited John there in the summer of 1972. As I do today, I found the country beautiful and its people warm and welcoming. However, in both positive and negative respects, it was a different country than it is today. There was more evidence of poverty in the 1970s (Wolfe, 2017). I observed more child malnutrition at that time. It was also a far less violent country than it is today (Wolfe, 2017). We moved about the country easily then, including by bus, which would not be recommended today.

Violence has increased to catastrophic rates in the last several years. The Peace Corps left El Salvador in 2016 due to security issues. The US government considers El Salvador too dangerous for

Peace Corps volunteers. In addition, the number of people seeking to escape violence from El Salvador, Guatemala, and Honduras has drastically increased in recent years (Wolfe, 2017).

On my return from El Salvador in 1972, I enrolled at the University of Chicago, completing a master's degree in international relations in 1974 and a PhD in human development (an interdisciplinary committee in anthropology, biology, psychology, and sociology) in 1982. Afterward, I worked full time for 15 years as a research psychologist on a longitudinal study of psychotic and mood disorders (Westermeyer, 1993; Westermeyer & Harrow, 1986, 1988; Westermeyer, Harrow & Marengo, 1991). I also completed a clinical psychology internship and became a licensed clinical psychologist. I am currently a professor of psychology at Adler University in Chicago where I have taught for over 27 years in the clinical psychology doctoral program.

John finished his law degree at Northwestern University following his return from El Salvador. He has been a practicing attorney in Chicago for over 45 years.

In the summer of 2003, 31 years after visiting El Salvador, John and I wanted to get involved in philanthropy. John wanted to reconnect with El Salvador and its people in particular. He contacted Mike Wise, director of the Peace Corps in El Salvador, who set up meetings with six groups in September 2003 to see if there was a good fit with our interests. We chose to work with two nonprofit organizations and are still working with one of them, Project Salvador, and their scholarship program today. We specifically chose to work with a scholarship program for adolescents and young adults who would not otherwise be able to obtain an education without a scholarship.

We have successfully raised funds for scholarships over the years. John works tirelessly for the scholarship program. His political skills and command of Spanish provide direct communications with students, families, and the in-country staff. In addition, John recruits friends and family to help. His wife, Peggy Kukankos, their children, Matt, Mary, and Ginney, other family members, and our many friends have played important roles in fundraising and organizing to keep the scholarship program going.

This book shares the stories of many students and others we have encountered over the years. These students remain in El Salvador despite violence and other challenges that prompt so many others to leave the country. In addition, the book presents information on the Project Salvador Scholarship Program, which gives many individuals opportunities for an education and employment that they otherwise would not have. The student's stories and those of others in El Salvador convey a difficult social and economic reality. However, they also tell of resilience and miraculous growth as these young people navigate difficult, formative years in which many have obtained an education, self-confidence, and employment. They remain in El Salvador to build a stronger country.

We have had the same professional driver, Don José, every year we have traveled throughout El Salvador. Don José, as well as the students, their families, and the in-country staff, knows when and where it is safe to travel within the country. However, a recent increase in violence makes it too dangerous for us to visit much of the country and most of the homes of students we frequently visited in the past. More communities have become controlled by street gangs at war with each other and government authorities over the time we have been visiting El Salvador (Martinez et al., 2016; Wolfe, 2017).

A sense of danger extends to people of all social classes that we meet, especially to impoverished people who fear gang violence and sometimes fear extrajudicial violent actions by police authorities. While wealthy and middle-class families can afford gated communities or ubiquitous armed guards to protect their homes and workplaces, the poor remain most vulnerable. The large number of people leaving El Salvador, Guatemala, and Honduras for asylum in the United States is no mystery to those familiar with the violence and extortion in the Northern Triangle region. For many immigrants, it is a stark matter of life or death to escape these countries (Semple, 2019a; Wolfe, 2017).

To better protect privacy, identifying information for all of the students and most other individuals discussed in this book has been altered. The names used are fictitious and some other identifying characteristics and places are altered to protect anonymity. Nevertheless, the stories are accurate for the individuals presented.

In addition, the various vignettes presented are not meant to be representative of all the Salvadoran people. Many Salvadorans thrive in safe middle- and upper-class neighborhoods or other communities

(Wolfe, 2017). The economy continues to expand most years. New roads, buildings, and businesses continue to grow, providing hope that further progress can be made. Nevertheless, these stories generally illustrate the conditions and events experienced by a large percentage of people living in poverty or experiencing extortion or violence. The reader should be cautioned that some stories describe traumatic incidents that may be upsetting for some individuals to read.

We continue to work with our colleague, Tony Gasbarro, a retired University of Alaska professor who founded the scholarship program in 1998, and our in-country colleagues, the Rivera family, as we have from the beginning of our scholarship program. The Rivera family is the heart and soul of the project. They provide continuous, monthly, face-to-face, in-country mentoring essential to the success of the program. Our association with the Rivera family began with Fatima and Humberto, who have worked for over 30 years on social justice projects in El Salvador. They are rare and noble individuals, devoting their lives to the betterment of the Salvadoran people.

Our involvement with the Rivera family continues today with their children, Beto, who directs the in-country program, his wife, Anna Valencia, his sisters Marisol, Anna Fatima, and Natalya as well as their spouses, friends, and other family's members including Carmen, Rolando, Tomas, Andres, and Arlene, who continue to provide support and mentoring for the students. The program could not succeed without them.

This book is written with the hope that US citizens and others gain a better understanding of the Salvadoran people and the conditions that drive many to desperate attempts for asylum in the United States or to internal displacements in their own country. Moreover, it is written with the hope of providing a better understanding of the Project Salvador Scholarship Program and other nongovernment organizations (NGOs) aid programs that help individuals who remain in El Salvador to escape the crippling cycle of poverty or to find alternative options to gang involvement.

The courage and resilience of Salvadoran scholarship students are representative of many children, adolescents, and young adults worldwide who struggle to improve their lives and attain an education despite wars, other types of violence, poverty, and oppressive conditions.

Sonia Wolfe (2017), a scholar on the politics of gang activities and gang control in El Salvador, writes:

> Research has shown that street gangs attract individuals who live in socially disorganized communities and face social exclusion, family problems and a lack of dignified education and job opportunities. . . . Gang control therefore requires an integrated approach based on prevention, law enforcement, and rehabilitation and reinsertion.

Solutions to the current crisis for the hopeful people from Central and South America presenting themselves for asylum at the

US southern border involve greater border security and judicial resources to adjudicate asylum cases as well as more safety from gang violence and extortion in their home countries that often precipitate immigration. However, as Wolfe (2017) suggests, the long-term solutions also involve "dignified education and job opportunities" that ultimately provide alternatives to street gang membership and pathways out of chronic poverty in their home countries. We believe our scholarship program provides such alternatives and pathways.

# CHAPTER 1
# THE GIRL BEGGING AT THE GAS STATION

> "The structures of social injustice are bringing a slow death to our poor." - Quote attributed to Saint Óscar Romero, Archbishop of San Salvador, painted on a house in El Salvador

> "Depending on one's estimate and the exact definition used, more than one billion people, and perhaps as many as 2.5 billion people, can be categorized as living in extreme poverty."
>
> - Jeffrey Sachs, *The Age of Sustainable Development*, 2015

Reading statistics on poverty is not the same as experiencing poverty. It is difficult for someone like me to understand the psychology and reality of poverty when raised in an affluent society such as the United States. What does it mean to live in poverty? Moreover, what are the personal reactions to viewing extreme poverty for the first time? El Salvador provided a variety of answers—especially on my initial trip in 2003 to begin our scholarship program.

I did not know what role I could play or what experiences or reactions I would encounter. I have lived a fairly privileged, middle-class existence and have had a rather comfortable life in the United States. Like most people from an economically developed country, I suspect, I personally had not met someone extremely poor living in a developing country before I traveled.

In addition, I am interested in the impact of childhood on adult development. Childhood is an especially vulnerable period of dependence on others. It encompasses a critical period of growth. I believe that if one is loved and nurtured well in childhood, the chances are pretty good that all will turn out well across the human life span. I wanted to be involved more with disadvantaged youth in some way. El Salvador, with its economic, social, and political problems, provided opportunities to make a difference in developing lives. Little did I know how true that was to become.

On our first day in the country in September 2003, I noticed a girl who was about 12 by a lake in Suchitoto. We had met the mayor of the town and his staff and were considering some type of involvement with them. As we were waiting for a sightseeing boat, the girl was laughing and playing, in the joys of childhood, oblivious to the problems of the world. This girl seemed poor and so, I assumed, had problems despite her laughter and joyous disposition. Then I thought: So what? Why can't the poor be as happy as or happier than anyone else?

On our return to the dock, she and two friends came up to us. They were talking and seemed very outgoing. I lamely asked her name. "Julia," she replied. My friend, John, gave her some money, but I didn't get caught up in the situation. I had my camera and was taking photographs of the lake and town. Somehow, I thought it inappropriate to take photos without permission. It was intuitively rude to me. It seemed doubly rude to try to document poverty at someone else's expense.

I got into the car and waved goodbye to her. She waved back. I suddenly felt bad about not giving her anything and not taking her photo. I was determined that would not occur again. As we drove through the town, I stopped to take a photo of artwork with a quote by Archbishop Saint Óscar Romero, a martyr for social justice, drawn on the side of a house. The quote read: "The structures of social injustice are bringing a slow death to our poor." How appropriate, I thought. Romero was assassinated in 1980 after speaking out on social justice issues. A 12-year civil war followed the assassination.

Before we met with the Peace Corps director the next day, I talked to Annie, a Peace Corps volunteer and administrator. She sponsored children in a small village where she volunteered on her own initiative. I asked her if John and I could sponsor one of her kids since we were looking for that kind of involvement. "Sure," she said and thanked me. I told her that it is something I needed to do—for myself.

I immediately felt better on giving her the donation. I trusted Annie, even though I had only known her for a day. There are people like that in life—people who seem extraordinary on a first meeting. John calls them "keepers." Annie's heart was in the right place. Her interactions with Salvadorans seemed natural. She put people at ease without patronizing them. A rare skill, I thought.

We got up early the next day to visit John's host family from his Peace Corps days. Our driver for sightseeing was Martín, the member of the family close in age to us. Although living a wild younger life, Martín, like so many others, miraculously evolved into a responsible husband and father. With Martín's support, his three children have had a good education, developed good careers, and now have middle-class jobs and families of their own. The lesson for me of Martín's life is that the reckless young have the time and opportunity to become something unexpected with aging. Immature adolescents, if given the opportunity, usually grow to mature adults.

Martín gave us a tour after meeting his extended family by their vacation property near the coast. He drove us around San Salvador to get a sense of the city. We saw miles of dilapidated slums and people living in impoverished conditions. We also saw great wealth, well-paved highways, busy shopping malls, government buildings, and beautiful middle- and upper-class neighborhoods. The sights, sounds, and smells of it all were overwhelming—especially observing extensive impoverished conditions for the first time. I wondered what life was like for people living in such neglected housing.

We stopped at a gas station to fill up. I got out of the car to stretch and get a better look at the location. Out of nowhere, a girl of about 11 walked up to me. Although no words were spoken, it was obvious she was poor and begging for money. She was lean and unkempt. Typical of Salvadoran girls, her features were dark, her eyes brown, and her face clear, well-proportioned, and framed by black hair. She wore slacks and a well-worn, red shirt. Her eyes were downcast and rarely met mine. She was striking to behold.

Remembering my lost opportunity for photos the previous day, I nodded at my camera and then her, requesting in this nonverbal way a photograph. She appeared to nod approval. I looked through the lens and took her photo. I then reached into my pocket for a dollar. Without any show of outward emotion, she received the gift with quiet dignity. John also gave her a dollar. Again, there was an emotionless, silent response from the girl. The meeting lasted a few seconds and no words were spoken.

As we drove out of the gas station, Martín exclaimed that she was crossing the street, a six-lane divided expressway with heavy car and truck traffic, in a dangerous fashion. John thought the same as Martín and commented on her quick, athletic movements. I turned to look. She miraculously dodged the traffic. The last I could see of her, she was running down an embankment toward tin "houses" with her $2 "fortune" to return home, probably to give it to her mother. I guessed the money, given its enormity, had to be brought home immediately. The houses were shabby, run-down slums. The dwellings did not seem fit for people.

As the last day of our visit approached, I felt I had to make another contribution before I left the country. I dropped off a donation with Humberto and Fatima Rivera, the Salvadoran couple we worked with. Later, I found out that we would be sponsoring three students in high school for one year. It does not cost much to support an adolescent in high school for one year in El Salvador. Again, the feeling of relief pressed in on me—I had done something in the face of such economic inequality.

For some reason, I could not shake the brief meeting with the girl begging at the gas station from my mind. The mystery of this simple girl was the focus of much thought on the plane ride home. On my return to Chicago, I immediately developed the many photographs I had taken on my trip at a local photo store. I was specifically looking for one photo—the girl begging at the gas station. I fumbled through many photos before finding it. The girl that I remember rarely making eye contact and never smiling was looking directly at me and smiling directly at me in the photo.

I was stunned and walked slowly out of the store into the bright sunlight feeling overwhelmed with emotion. I was powerfully affected by this photo—this girl—and yet had no idea why. As I walked, tears spontaneously gushed from my eyes and could not be stopped. I sobbed deeply—sobbed as never before and as never since. No matter what losses or disappointments I had experienced in my life, I could not remember a more intense crying. It physically shook me.

The outpouring of affect surprised me. What was happening to me? Why this reaction? I ticked off possible explanations: The girl? The situation? Could it be a delayed emotional reaction to seeing extreme poverty in a "developing" country up close? Had I kept feelings of what I had observed in check until now? Veterans of poverty interventions told me of similar initial feelings on seeing gross poverty or experiencing vicarious trauma for the first time.

Had unconscious reactions surfaced with this photograph? What affected me more than anything was the gift of the unexpected smile—really the only gift she could give me. The sobbing did not abate quickly but continued out of control for some time. It was following by deep, perplexing relief as to what happened and why.

For whatever reason, she affected me more than I could say. Again, on the next day, and the next day, I cried deeply when I thought about her. It was a chance encounter lasting seconds without any words being spoken. Yet the impact was palpable and beyond anything else experienced on the trip or, it seemed, in my life. The injustice of it all, I thought. What chance does she have in life? The stale fact of a billion or more people in the world living in extreme poverty was made real in the persona of one young girl.

I expressed an interest to my friend, Mike Jenkins, in finding the girl on a subsequent trip to El Salvador 9 months later. Mike was the in-country director of one of the NGOs that we worked with. He and his wife, Susie, both former Peace Corps volunteers, were to become our great friends in El Salvador. Initially, it was difficult for Mike to find the girl, but he persisted. With the photo I had taken, Mike returned to the cluster of homes to inquire about her. As last she was found. Maria was 11 years old when I first met her.

Maria was one of 12 children living with their parents in a tin dwelling on public land. Over the next few years we tried to help her and her siblings, particularly the youngest daughter, Adrian, who was a few days old when Mike located the family. She had been born prematurely and was markedly underweight. It was questionable if the infant would survive. The first year of life is an extremely vulnerable period among the economically disadvantaged of the world who experience a much higher infant mortality rate than the wealthy of the world (LeVine & LeVine, 2016). Mike intervened and regularly brought baby formula to the household for many weeks. Fortunately, Adrian survived as she gradually gained weight and strength.

Despite providing resources to fund Maria's education, efforts to help her complete school were unsuccessful. Although she stayed in school and off the streets for a couple of years, Maria entered a common-law marriage at age 13 with her 15-year-old boyfriend, Alex, and dropped out of school. Her parents initially opposed the common-law marriage and physically restrained her in their home to prevent her from meeting with Alex. Maria, however, ultimately found a way for them to reunite.

Maria had a child at age 13 and another at age 16 with Alex. She was voluntarily sterilized at age 16. Although Maria's mother chose to have 12 children, explaining that it was "God's will," Maria chose to limit her family to two children just after the birth of her second child. Jeffrey Sachs (2015) and others have reported that women, in both developing and developed countries, are choosing to limit the size of their families.

Maria experienced periods of homelessness with her first child and was physically abused by Alex. She eventually returned to live with her parents and, with periodic separations from Alex, continued to raise her two children. By all indications, Maria was a devoted mother. Her daughter and son are now older than Maria was when we initially met her. On last contact through Mike three years ago, Maria, then in her mid-20s, was working part time as a secretary and striving to keep her two young children in school.

I have now made over 35 trips to El Salvador since 2003. I have become aware of many more problematic situations than that which I initially observed with Maria: terrible stories of trauma, hunger, child neglect and maltreatment, and street gang violence, including extortion and murder. Yet I have had nothing near the same reaction I had with the girl begging at the gas station so many years ago.

As "nothing human is foreign to us," my understanding of my reactions after that initial visit to El Salvador is that, with time and experience, we get used to most new situations with which we are unfamiliar, including unpleasant or difficult experiences. I have observed this phenomenon in clinical work. Initial vicarious trauma experienced with clients usually loses its disruptive power as clinicians "adapt" with repeated exposure to more clients and better defend themselves in various ways to the traumatized experiences told to them by clients (Herman, 1997/2015).

Another lesson learned is the miracle of changes that becomes apparent in doing long-term follow-ups with the same people and the remarkable development that can occur over many years. Maria, the 11-year-old girl begging at the gas station and early school dropout, is now a devoted, loving, 20-something mother of two healthy children who has given opportunities to her children that she did not have. She has attained enough skills in school to do light secretarial work. Her two young children attend school. Perhaps the few years Maria spent in primary school had a larger, positive impact on her life than can be measured. Maria survives. I marvel at the resilience and resourcefulness of those living in deep poverty.

# CHAPTER 2
# INTERVENTIONS: WHAT WORKS?

> "Change comes when men see the benefits of women's power—not just what women can do that men cannot, but a quality of relationship that comes in an equal partnership that cannot come in a hierarchical relationship, a sense of bonding, of belonging, of community, solidarity and wholeness."
>
> - Melinda Gates, *The Moment of Lift*, 2019

Social justice activities involve this important question: What is the most effective way to help others? As I have learned over the years, interventions have the potential to be deleterious or irrelevant as well as helpful.

The 12th-century Jewish philosopher, Maimonides, struggled with questions of giving and wrote of eight levels of charity or philanthropy (Maimonides, 2006). At the highest level was giving in a way that helped people help themselves. Did it empower them to where they could continue for years on their own and eventually not need their benefactor?

As John and I embarked on philanthropic possibilities in El

Salvador in September 2003, the Peace Corps director, Mike Wise, put us in touch with six groups. We chose to work with two of the groups. One group was directed by Mike and Susie Jenkins, former Peace Corps volunteers who were introduced in the last chapter. Upon returning to El Salvador as a retired couple in 2002, they became larger-than-life figures in the village in which they have worked for over 17 years. They have been involved in a variety of social justice activities, including medical missions, house construction, water projects, and a scholarship program. One of the great benefits of living for something larger than the self is that you meet wonderful people along the way. Mike and Susie are such people. They became close, lifelong friends to John and me.

We first met Mike and Susie in Wise's office in San Salvador in September 2003. Director Wise explained to us the difficulties of interventions to help the poor in developing countries. Based on decades of experience, Wise said that many types of interventions he had seen may result in deleterious outcomes. An authoritarian approach in which an outside force imposes "the answer" on communities may lead to regressions or resentments among those it seeks to help. If everything is done for them, a sense of powerlessness or ineffectiveness may creep in, sometimes to the point of increased dependency on a more powerful organization. Wise maintained he had seen this happen too often in his years as a Peace Corps administrator in various countries. I thought then that successful interventions to address social justice issues were not easily achieved.

At this point in the conversation, Mike piped up: "I have a solution for that problem." Mr. Mike, as he is fondly known to both US volunteers and Salvadorans, explained that he never engages in a community development project unless the people in the community support the project.

Mike said that the community must invest in the project with planning, time, and resources. In this way, interventions are more likely to empower rather than devalue individuals. Mike explained, "Unless they (the community) are fully involved, we don't get involved." We can assume that people in the community know best how to improve their lives. If truly committed to their project, they are more likely to be motivated, energized, and dedicated to its success. Maimonides, I think, would approve.

I am reminded of Mike's words in the text of several books on interventions and philanthropy. For example, Melinda Gates (2019), in her wise book, *The Moment of Lift*, describes how real change in Africa communities struggling with issues of child marriage and genital cutting needs to come from internal deliberations rather than external coercion. She describes how small-group discussions led women to voice their objections to such practices and to persuade others to not subject their daughter to such actions despite the time-honored traditions of their culture. Since external threats were not effective, the minds of the people themselves had to change for there to be an effective, long-term end to these practices (Gates, 2019).

Over the years, projects in El Salvador, such as microlending programs (starting by Muhammad Yunus in Bangladesh) and Habitat for Humanity, well exemplified Mike's and Gates' recommendations for success. Small loans in microcredit projects sometimes had a major impact on a budding entrepreneur building a business. A $50 or $100 loan could provide a significantly increased, sustained income for a family. Similarly, with Habitat for Humanity, people must own the land on which their houses are built, and they must put "sweat equity" into the building of the house. This process more likely ensures commitment to the home, pride of ownership, and connection to the community.

John and I decided that our largest commitment in El Salvador would be to a scholarship program. Our involvement in this program has increased over the years. The scholarships go to poor but talented, motivated adolescents and young adults who would otherwise be unable to afford their education. John and I thought we could not go wrong with a commitment to education. Investing in human capital reaps benefits not only for the individual but for their family and community as well. An education continues to give for generations through the achievements of the individual and their impact on children, grandchildren, and the wider community.

Consequently, John and I also chose to work with the Project Salvador Scholarship Program. We are still involved in this program today. This scholarship program was developed in 1998 by Tony Gasbarro, a retired University of Alaska professor and former Peace Corps volunteer, along with Humberto and Fatima Rivera.

Humberto and Fatima are originally from Ecuador. They have worked as a husband/wife team on social justice projects in El

Salvador for over 30 years. Their organization has been involved in housing, scholarships, agricultural development projects, and other community development activities too numerous to mention. They were forced to leave the country during the Salvadoran Civil War for a 4-year period in which they worked on similar social justice activities in Guatemala.

We started sponsoring three students with Humberto and Fatima in 2003. The students we sponsor are typically from the *campo* (the rural country) with no model of academic success in their families or community. Other than a few students who have a sibling in the program, they are the first members of their family to attend college. Most of their parents did not attend high school. Their primary and high school education is generally inferior to the education received by children of wealthy families in the cities, who often attend well-resourced, private schools. Few adolescents from the rural, lower social classes finish high school. Rarely do they have an opportunity to succeed in college and beyond. About 5% of Salvadorans graduate from college.

Essential to success in the scholarship program is an in-country mentorship program. More than anyone, Fatima Rivera supplied that crucial role in our first few years in El Salvador. Fatima was like a mother to our first three female students, Cindy, Lesia, and Sara. Fatima visited them frequently, advising them on study habits and advocating for them to school authorities.

Fatima opened her home and her heart to these students from the campo. Most importantly, she provided them reasons to believe that girls from the campo could be the first in their families to graduate from the university and have a career. This was not the norm for young girls in their cultural setting. It became obvious that a strong, consistent mentoring program was essential to the success of students who did not have the benefits of a quality education or of financial, social, and family support.

After a lifetime of social activism, Fatima and Humberto retired in 2014 and returned to Ecuador. Their work continues through their adult children and others who now administer the scholarship program. These colleagues include their son, Beto, who directs the in-country program, and several other family members and friends. They regularly and selflessly meet at least once a month with each group of students for consultation and training while continuously monitoring their academic progress.

One example of this continuous mentoring involves book discussion groups starting by Beto's sister, Marisol. Marisol previously worked as a flight attendant and speaks excellent English. As she became involved in her own book discussion group, she felt that such discussions would be a great way for students to improve their reading and speaking skills as well as develop a love of learning. Marisol bought books for the students and organized monthly discussion groups. The books included Antoine de Saint-Exupery's *The Little Prince,* Franz Kafka's *The Metamorphosis,* John Steinbeck's *Of Mice and Men,* William Shakespeare's *Romeo and Juliet,* and Gabriel García Marquez's *Chronicle of a Death Foretold.* The students loved the books and monthly discussions. The activity spurred on the love of reading and improved group morale and support.

Some students face special problems, for which support and counseling may be necessary. They may be forced to suspend their education for a time to work and provide food for their families. Family members may experience illnesses that require students' attention at home. Other issues may involve a death in the family, parental abandonment, domestic violence, gang extortion, or financial crises.

Another problem may involve an inadequate education that they may have received, which may require remediation or advocacy on behalf of students to school authorities. After graduation, students may need consultation on résumés, job searches, and interviews. The Rivera family reviews grades and provides continuous support and mentoring on a variety of topics in monthly meetings.

The scholarship program allows students to take the primary responsibility for their education. First, students are selected for their good grades in primary school or high school, motivation to obtain an education, and financial need. Second, they must maintain good grades to continue receiving the scholarship. We emphasize that the scholarship is not a gift but rather an award they have earned and must work to maintain. This sets up a different psychological relationship. We are partners in the enterprise, not a distant authority doling out remittances to those less powerful. It feels right. I think Mike, Gates, and Maimonides would agree.

In addition, scholarships provide easily defined and measured outcomes, which is a major advantage in evaluating the effectiveness of our program. Good grades and high graduation rates are accurate and valid criteria of success for the program. Moreover, we continue to monitor and meet with program's alumni years after graduation to assess paid employment outcomes and their impact on families and communities.

Rosita was one of our first scholarship students to attend high school and then college in the mid-2000s. She was one of five sisters raised by their mother, a single parent, who supported the family selling fruit in the public marketplace. Rosita struggled to graduate from college. She needed to take time off from school twice to support herself and her family with temporary jobs. Nevertheless, she did graduate after years of hard work. Rosita is now employed as a high school teacher, a much-needed occupation in El Salvador.

This job provides Rosita with a good income to help her family. In addition to increased income, we have seen changes in Rosita over the last 14 years. She is more confident, articulate, responsible, and hopeful about the world and her possibilities for success. In brief, we saw her grow spiritually and as a person. The larger world of ideas, books, and opportunities was opened to her.

Education further impacts the family and community. If Rosita can achieve success in her education and career, other members of her family and community (especially young girls) are more likely to perceive they too can accomplish those goals.

Not so surprisingly, Rosita's younger sister, Cruz, followed her into the scholarship program and graduated in December 2018 from college with a degree in business administration. Cruz now works in the accounting department at a large business firm. Their mother, who did not progress beyond third grade and can barely read or write, is proud of her daughters. Today, other girls and young women in their community are more open to the possibilities of an education and the benefits of a career for themselves.

# CHAPTER 3
# DOCTOR SARA

..............................................................

"My scholarship and education have been the most beautiful experiences in my life."

"I never doubted myself. I was going to reach inside of myself and find whatever it took to graduate and become a doctor."

-Dr. Sara, a 29-year-old alumna of the scholarship program

Over the years, scholarship students and others have told us stories of extortion, beatings, threats, and murder in El Salvador, which were reasons to either leave the country or to make some adjustment and remain with family in the country. Sara is one example.

We were supporting Sara's cousin, Gilda, in 2003, when she dropped out of school to have her first child. At age 13, Sara proactively pursued a scholarship with us. When we arrived to visit her region in early 2004, Sara had been waiting for hours by the road with Felicia, her mother, to request our help to obtain an education. She was determined to succeed—and the years since our first meeting verified that determination. Sara was not to be denied an education.

Sara never knew her father, who abandoned the family soon

after her birth. Typical of many families, her mother struggled to raise Sara and her two brothers alone by farming a small plot of land. Felicia raised cows and gradually improved the property, increasing her income over the years we visited the family. Felicia committed to helping her daughter achieve her dream. Sara later commented: "My mother has been a great support for me. I grew up with only my mother at my side. My mother studied until the eighth grade and could not continue due to the lack of economic resources."

Given that Sara had no role models, particularly female ones, it is remarkable that she developed the goal of becoming a physician and fought so diligently to obtain it. Sara said her motivation to become a physician grew from the medical problems she had witnessed as a child that could not be addressed due to the lack of medical services. She described a neighbor who died because there was no physician available. Sara wanted to correct this deficiency.

Sara sacrificed daily for her education and thrived in school. She became a star student. Within three years of starting the scholarship program in high school, Sara won an award based on her academic performance. Out of scores of high school students, she won a first-place prize: a computer. Sara had a secret weapon to explain her academic achievements: She was intellectually gifted.

Within a few years, Sara was accepted to medical school at age 18, the typical age for entering medical school in El Salvador. Medical school is at least an 8-year academic program that includes college courses.

Sara struggled at first and had to repeat some classes. She

studied by candlelight each night and spent hours each day commuting to the university. Unlike other young women her age, she initially avoided involvement with a *novio* (boyfriend), which may have led to an early marriage and parenthood or may have detracted from her studies. She fought like hell and sacrificed much to succeed. When asked later if she ever doubted that she would become a physician, Sara responded, "No, I never doubted myself. I was going to reach inside of myself and find whatever it took to graduate and become a doctor."

The odds of her succeeding were not in her favor due to her earlier educational environment and lack of family resources. Sara was educated in rural schools. Consequently, her education was inferior to her richer, better educated fellow students from the city. Nevertheless, Sara was bright and assertive. When necessary, she aggressively lobbied us for funds she needed to buy books and study materials. Although she needed an extra year to complete her degree, she was persistent.

Furthermore, Fatima Rivera, the in-country staff member at that time, continually mentored, encouraged, and supported Sara. Fatima met with medical school officials to advocate for her. She opened her home to Sara to provide a place of nurturance, safety, and love. Sara, a disadvantaged girl from the campo, survived the high attrition rate in the early years of medical school.

In the summer of 2016, we took then 25-year-old Sara to speak to 13 high school girls who were entering the scholarship program and were about the same age as Sara when she started with us 12 years previously. The mere presence of Sara, an example of success they sought to emulate, spoke far more eloquently than John or I could. Sara's message could be summed up in the following few words she spoke to them: "You must be strong. No matter what comes—be strong." Yes, I thought, throughout the years of her education in the scholarship program, Sara demonstrated strength at each step of the process.

Two months later, in September, however, Sara faced her greatest challenge. For about 10 years, we often visited Sara's family home in the country where they made a living in subsistence farming. Then, over a 2- to 3-year period, street gangs moved into the community, which made it impossible for the staff or us to visit the area.

In response, the police and army authorities developed a partial, temporary presence in the community and killed a gang member. In retaliation, gang members killed one of Sara's cousins who they suspected had informed the authorities. Later, gang members went to the farm and told Sara's mother that the family must pay *renta* (extortion money) or Sara and one of her brothers would be killed. Such extortions often occur in gang-controlled territories throughout the Northern Triangle countries of Central America.

The in-country staff suggested that Sara may have been targeted by gang members in the area partly over envy of her success. The community knew she was making her way through medical school.

All knew the death threat was serious, putting Sara and her brother in grave danger. The amount of money demanded by the gang, however, was too exorbitant to be paid. If paid, gangs typically return for more extortion money. The family immediately realized, as many others extorted in Central America do, that the situation was extremely perilous as they could not afford to pay the extortion demand. The family immediately packed up and left the area to live with relatives in a safer part of El Salvador, abandoning the property they worked to develop over many years.

When we visited and saw Sara a few months later in late November, she rightly looked frightened and unsure of what she should do. A cousin in the United States urged Sara to flee El Salvador for the United States as soon as possible and offered to pay the $8,000 to $9,000 fee charged by "coyotes" (individuals paid to transport people to the United States) to make the trip.

Like many other Central Americans, Sara had two choices: stay and risk death by the gangs or perilously attempt to cross the US border and reach safety. Leaving El Salvador would mean the end of Sara's chances for a medical degree and the loss of years of a hard-fought education. The dream of being a physician would be lost. Moreover, the trip through Guatemala and Mexico would be physically perilous with no guarantee of success. We have heard stories of Central American immigrants who are killed or injured on their way to America through Mexico. Coyotes may take money from people and then disappear. Many people attempting to escape extortion and violence are turned back along the way while few enter the United States (Semple, 2019a). Furthermore, life in the United States likely would involve persistent, low-wage, menial jobs with a lack of opportunity for advancement and the constant threat of deportation back to El Salvador.

By the time we visited again the following January, Sara and her family had found a safe home in another part of El Salvador. Sara, with staff encouragement and support, decided to stay in the country. She started her medical internship, which was to run for 2 years preceding her graduation. When we saw Sara then, she looked much better and more relaxed.

John and I visited Sara again 1.5 years later in a city where she was working in a medical clinic as part of her internship. We met Sara and her medical supervisor, Dr. García, in Sara's office. García praised Sara, saying in her many years of mentoring interns, Sara was one of her best. She explained that Sara was competent, reliable, and stayed long hours to make sure her patients were cared for completely. John and I beamed with pride as felt by parents when hearing about a successful child.

Dr. García also told us that many patients attending the clinic specifically asked for Sara. We took photos and told them what an honor it was for us to be there. We felt so grateful and fortunate to be associated with Sara, who John and I think of as a daughter. In turn, Sara thinks of us as fathers she never had and calls us the "angels" in her life.

John attended Sara's graduation from medical school about 9 months later in March 2019, with Felicia and Sara's novio, Ronaldo, who she recently met at the university. The Rivera family joined them afterward at a restaurant to enjoy a celebration dinner with many happy toasts.

A few months later, Sara opened her own clinic with two friends in a medium-sized town in El Salvador. Ronaldo helped raise $2,000 to adequately supply the new clinic with necessary medical equipment. Soon after opening, however, gang members in the area came to the clinic demanding extortion money. The clinic had to be closed. The investment money was lost.

Dr. Sara, as strong as ever, was undaunted and pursued other options. She got a job at a private hospital about a 40-minute bus ride from her home. There, she is acquiring additional clinical experience and is serving the community as a physician just as she had dreamed of doing in her childhood. Most importantly, Sara and Felicia feel great satisfaction in Dr. Sara's medical care of others. Felicia described how following medical treatment, patients would call Dr. Sara and say, "Thank you. I am better."

Dr. Sara is considering a medical residency in surgery in the next two years, which would open new job opportunities for her. She also is now in a better position to financially help her mother and two younger brothers. Moreover, Dr. Sara has not abandoned her goal of opening her own medical clinic, but her plans are on hold for now.

I expect new obstacles will be thrown in Dr. Sara's path in the future. But given her fortitude, persistence, maturity, and resilience, which I have observed over many years, I also expect Dr. Sara to successfully overcome them and turn negatives into positives. Dr. Sara will not be vanquished. I am grateful to know her, to be her *padrino* (godfather), and to have her as my friend.

# CHAPTER 4
# THE DISAPPEARANCE OF A DAUGHTER

..............................................................

> "She walks in beauty, like the night
> Of cloudless climes and starry skies;
> And all that's best of dark and bright
> Meet in her aspect and her eyes...
>
> The smiles that win, the tints that glow,
> But tell of days in goodness spent,
> A mind at peace with all below,
> A heart whose love is innocent!"
> - Lord Byron, "She Walks in Beauty"

On a Saturday evening in January a few years ago, Anna, age 20, her friend Rebeca, age 28, and Rebeca's 3-year-old daughter, Teresa, left their homes to attend a social event in another community. The two young women were good friends, living close to each other along a dirt path in a dilapidated urban slum area of San Salvador. Street gangs control many of the neighborhoods where the poor reside. Travel from one neighborhood to another can be risky as it may be necessary to cross gang boundaries.

The night turned to morning, and they did not return home.

Following a brief stay, I had left El Salvador the day after the women disappeared. The week after I left, Mike Jenkins called with the news of the disappearance. I was shocked. I had met Anna and her family on many occasions with Mike over a 10-year period, but I had not seen them for about 2 years. I knew Anna as a polite, friendly, young woman who was close to her family and worked strenuously to succeed in school. She, like most other young adults I know in the country, did her best to survive in a culture of poverty and violence. The disappearance appalled me and made no sense. I needed to know what happened to Anna.

After a few more days, Teresa was found alone on a street in San Salvador. A note with her family's address was pinned to her clothing. There were no other words on the note. The child was returned to her extended family who were anxious for additional information on the disappearance and why Teresa was returned while the two young women were not.

Months passed and still Anna and Rebeca couldn't be found. The police presumed they were dead. Unfortunately, such disappearances occur too frequently in El Salvador. Many parents keep their children indoors most of the day to avoid gang recruitment, extortion, or violent attacks.

John and I first met Anna's family through Mike and Susie. I often accompanied Mike as he traveled through his village and the surrounding area outside of San Salvador to work on community development projects. Mike is smart, pragmatic, and compassionate. He chose to work with Anna's family, which included Anna's two sisters and her mother, Christina.

Christina raised her three daughters and earns her living selling candy and gum at a congested street intersection. She rises early to travel downtown to buy supplies to sell for the day. Then for hours she, frequently with one or two of her daughters, stands by the highway, selling items to passing motorists and earning a few dollars each day to support her family. Christina works and sacrifices daily for her most precious possession—her children.

Mike met Christina while she was working, and they struck up a friendship. Seeing the goodness of this family as well as their lack of financial resources, Mike arranged through John and other friends to financially support Julia, Christina's oldest daughter, in completing her education. Julia successfully graduated from high school and obtained an associate degree in college in hopes of better supporting the family.

Christina's home is located among small, tin dwellings in an area for the urban poor who settle and build huts on public or unused land. It has a dirt floor and comprises one room separated into two sections by blankets slung across a rope. There is no electricity and little space. Typical of Salvadoran hospitality, however, Christina and her daughters are most welcoming on each visit. We have watched Anna grow from an 8-year-old child to a beautiful, 20-year-old woman.

As violence increased and street gangs extended their territory into the family's neighborhood, it became too dangerous for Mike to visit Christina's home. He must now call to arrange meetings with

Christina in public, safe locations. Mike called Christina as soon as he learned of the disappearance. Christina was heartbroken when Anna failed to return home on that January evening. Anna was a recent high school graduate who started to study nursing at the university.

As time passed, not a trace of information about the two missing women came forward. The police were not optimistic that they would be found. Evidently, missing individuals are not rare in El Salvador, and, according to the police, are seldom found after they are missing for a couple of days. The authorities have little resources or time to devote to solving the large number of disappearances and murders among the poor. Occasionally, unidentified corpses are found in deserted locations such as abandoned wells. The police assumed the young women were murdered and their bodies disposed in unmarked graves. Murders are committed with impunity, and few murders are investigated or solved in El Salvador (Wolfe, 2017).

Rumors circulated as to what may have happened and why. One narrative suggested that Rebeca had street gang affiliations. Another suggested that the two young women had gone to a party in a rival gang's territory and so were trespassers who paid for their offense with their lives. Although murders may occur for a variety of reasons, many murders in El Salvador involve warfare among the primary gangs that engage in violent conflict. Gangs control their territory carefully.

Christina traveled to the area where the women disappeared in an attempt to gather information. But no one knew anything—or would not say anything for fear of retribution.

Although a definitive explanation for the disappearance is still not forthcoming, I do know that Anna was an innocent, young woman without gang affiliations and was trying to improve her life and help her family against great odds. Unlike much gang activity in the United States, gang violence is more likely to claim the lives of innocent people in El Salvador (Ortiz, 2017). For me, Anna's life is representative of other young people in El Salvador and the world over who reflect the beauty of youthful innocence well described in Lord Byron's poetry.

The injustice of it all is overpowering. It is difficult for me to imagine what may have taken place in the last horrible moments of Anna's life. Disappearances of young women in poverty-ridden, gang-infested areas may involve gang rape or torture. What might 3-year-old Teresa have felt or observed in losing her mother without the language ability to express her trauma?

Christina was devastated and inconsolable as she frantically searched for her daughter and an explanation for the disappearance. A deep depression sank in when she realized her daughter likely would not be found. In desperation, notices were put in the newspaper and rewards offered for any information on Anna's disappearance. Unknown individuals called offering information if Christina first paid the reward. A reward of $100, which Christina had great difficulty collecting, was paid in vain. The callers cruelly took advantage of Christina's grief. They had no information to sell.

Some months later, a mass grave of murdered victims was found in another part of the country. Christina was able to examine the corpses to see if her daughter was among them. She could not go alone to visit the murder victims, so she requested that close relatives go with her. Christina was traumatized by the trip. She did not recognize her daughter among the decaying corpses.

Christina was left with no answers. The police authorities have long since abandoned the meager efforts they made to locate Anna. Christina turned to the care of her two remaining daughters, increasingly fearful that they too will be taken from her. She was reluctant to let them out of her sight. Her mind wandered to all sorts of possibilities in the absence of definitive information. She wondered if the disappearance was related to envious competitors selling goods along the highway.

A brother urged her either to stay in the safety of her home most of the day or leave the neighborhood where unknown individuals may have played a malevolent role in the disappearance. Christina stayed in her home—she has nowhere else to go or turn to for help. Her grief is profound, and she cannot sleep or eat sufficiently. She misses her daughter terribly.

Anna's story is similar to many other untold stories of victims of violence in Central America and elsewhere. Today, few NGO volunteers venture into marginal or gang-controlled neighborhoods. Corruption is more likely in impoverished societies where money is more enticing, and people have fewer options to escape dangerous neighborhoods. Many fear the police may be corrupted by gang bribes and may provide information to gang members if they turn to them for help. The fear of potential gang retaliation paralyzes many individuals. Gang members themselves pay a high price in this insidious process as they suffer a high probability of early death or extended prison time.

POST-SCRIPT

••••••••••••••••••••

Three years later Christina still lives in the same place with her two daughters and still sells candy and gum along the highway to survive. She lives without any information on what became of Anna. Her youngest daughter now has graduated from high school, and Mike has arranged to sponsor this daughter for further education with funds he raised from friends and his personal savings. The youngest daughter, Phoenix, has decided to study nursing at the university, the same noble, helping profession chosen by her murdered, older sister.

# CHAPTER 5
# "PEACE BE WITH YOU"

....................................................

"Anyone who has had an experience of mystery knows that there is a dimension of the universe that is not that which is available to his senses."- Joseph Campbell, *The Power of Myth with Bill Moyers*, 1991

"Positive emotion, meditation, and spiritual experience cannot be disentangled."
- George E. Vaillant, *Aging Well*, 2002

Mythology scholar Joseph Campbell discusses spiritually powerful, transformative events that he termed epiphanies. Epiphanies, according to Campbell (1991), are the aesthetic experiences of beholding phenomenon, which is one of radiance or rapture in living that transcends the ordinary. An epiphany is a profoundly spiritual experience of the mysteries of life beyond the senses that transcends ordinary, everyday experiences. An epiphany for me occurred over 10 years ago at an orphanage church in El Salvador.

Mike Jenkins was a regular visitor to the orphanage, La Comunidad de Oscar Arnulfo Romero (COAR Peace Mission, Inc.).

He placed individuals from his village who were in need of special care at the orphanage: a child suffering from fetal alcohol syndrome, an adolescent sexually abused for several years by her stepfather, others in need of safety and love. The orphanage has taken in homeless, impoverished, abused, or neglected children over the years.

I have witnessed the good done by COAR. COAR takes children living in the shadows of life and gives them an experience of warmth, safety, and the opportunity for an education. COAR also has a large grade school and high school that children from the neighborhood attend alongside the orphans.

For over 14 years at COAR, I have sponsored two siblings, Nancy and Nestor, who were abandoned by their mother as infants. When Nancy was 6 and Nestor was 8, their father was murdered by thieves on his way home from work. The thieves demanded his paycheck from work that day and killed him when he refused.

Because the siblings' grandparents did not have the resources to care for the children, they were placed at COAR. Nestor eventually returned to live with his grandparents after several years. Nancy recently graduated from the COAR high school. At age 20, she currently lives independently with other adult students and studies psychology at a university through a COAR scholarship.

I visited Nancy once or twice a year for 14 years at COAR. For the first few years, she seemed depressed and rarely smiled. However, with the good care provided by COAR, I witnessed her transformation. For the last several years, she was a smiling and outgoing young woman who was usually enjoying the company of friends.

For the past 7 years, I also sponsored 12-year-old Erick at COAR. The authorities found Erick wandering the streets of San Salvador, homeless and alone, at 5 years old. His family could not be located. COAR took him in and now provides a home and an education for him. Due to early life neglect, Erick is intellectually challenged.

When I ask Erick his dream for the future, he responds that he hopes to be a soldier one day. This dream has not changed over the years. I wonder if soldiers played a helpful role for Erick somewhere along the way.

The overall development I observed in Nancy, Erick, and other traumatized or discarded children at COAR has been miraculous.

On the day of my epiphany, Mike and I visited several children at the orphanage that Mike personally knew from his village. Afterward, we attended a Catholic Mass in the orphanage's large church. For some unknown reason, the participants in the Mass that day were primarily 5- to 7-year-old children. The kindergarten or first-grade classes from the orphanage school were attending church together. Aside from Mike, me, and the children's teachers, there were few adults in the church.

The event that so affected me occurred at the Mass' peace greeting. For those who have not been to a Catholic Mass, the peace greeting occurs toward the end of the service. You shake hands with those surrounding you, front to back and side to side, and typically say "Peace be with you." This is always my favorite part of the Mass. It gives me a warm feeling and epitomizes a community of goodwill. Whatever brings together those seeking solace or worship, a brief warm wish and handshake, in my previous experiences, instills a spiritual feeling of connectedness to all. Strangers and acquaintances alike meet, touch, and speak kindly to one another.

Mike and I sat toward the back of a church full of small children as the peace greeting approached. When the moment came, as if on cue, pandemonium broke loose and small children exploded in movement. With shrieks of joy, the children ran toward the few adults in the church. Taking me by surprise, about 20 children rushed toward Mike and me to excitedly express the peace greeting.

Their style of expressing peace, however, was not the usual, formal, ritualized handshake in so many other Catholic Masses that I have attended in both the United States and El Salvador. Rather, their peace greeting was an *abrazo* (hug), something so characteristic of Latin culture. Mike and I were surrounded by a sea of little arms reaching up to us for hugs. What followed was a joyous frenzy of hugs for 1 or 2 minutes—followed by a dash by the children returning to their places in the church.

The experience was overwhelmingly positive for me. I'm guessing that all people have felt the joyous, wonderful experience of a child's spontaneous hug at some moment in life. Here, there was a succession of hug after hug from a menagerie of laughing, joyous kids. As the hugs progressed, I was deeply affected by their exuberance and, in spite of myself, I started laughing along with them. I have never before or since had such an enchanting, spiritual experience during a religious gathering. This is what a spiritual experience in religious rituals should be but so rarely is—joyous, spontaneous, and fun.

It was a radiant, spiritual feeling, or in terms of a religious metaphor, the Christ—please, dear reader, substitute any religious figure or spiritual metaphor of your choosing—in human nature coming through. I can't shake the thought that this spiritual connection is what Jesus must have meant the Mass to be when he said, "Do this in memory of me." Revelation occurs in interpersonal connections rather than in religious rituals and scripture. It was doubly meaningful in this context in a child's hug. I rarely go to church. But if all too stodgy, serious religious services could be as sublime as what I experienced that day, then sign me up.

Later I reflected that many of those children had been abandoned or badly treated in their young lives, like Nancy, Nestor, and Erick. I indirectly knew some of their life stories, which included trauma or neglect. Many of these children lived without the daily loving touch of parents in their lives. Love from others is a necessity for all of us—especially little kids. A pediatrician friend of mine told me that newborn infants die if not touched by human hands. We have evolved as social beings that thrive on the touch, sight, sound, smell, and closeness of others. Our brains are designed to be comforted by other human beings.

These kids wanted to be hugged and exchange a greeting. The peace greeting gave them social permission to rush to the few adults to get the hugs they craved. Like me, they seemed to find the peace greeting the most meaningful experience in the Mass—the high point of their day.

Conversely, I needed their hugs too. They meant a great deal to me. This experience was a positive and joyous moment in my life. It has forever stayed with me as a most wonderful, spiritual experience. Pure joy!

For George Vaillant (2008), positive emotions (such as joy, love, hope, faith, compassion, forgiveness, awe) are synonymous with spirituality, are more important than negative emotions (such as depression, disgust, and anger), and are increasing over our evolutionary development.

An important question is how to put such joy and other positive affects in our lives on a more regular basis. Epiphanies can't be forced or intentionally manufactured. Rather, we can put ourselves in situations where they may be more likely to occur or be open to such rare moments when they do occur. According to Campbell (1991), epiphanies go beyond the mundane and reveal the spiritual possibilities of life. They may include the beautiful often found in nature and relationships or the monstrous that opens us up to the other or inspires awe that transcends the senses.

Although not exactly identical to epiphanies, joy in altruistic social activism in some ways may be closely related to them. Mohandas Gandhi (1957) argues in his enlightened autobiography that all social activism must be done in a spirit of joy. He writes:

Service can have no meaning unless one takes pleasure in it.

When it is done for show or for fear of public opinion, it stunts the man and crushes his spirit. Service which is rendered without joy helps neither the servant nor the served. But all other pleasures and possessions pale into nothingness before service which is rendered in a spirit of joy. (Gandhi, 1957)

Gandhi suggests that an altruistic orientation may take time to develop. He also indicates that one intentionally may develop sincere altruism. He describes caring for the basic needs of his brother-in-law for a time before his death. Although it was initially difficult, Gandhi found it a joyous activity as the weeks and months went by. He missed caring for his brother-in-law after he died (Gandhi, 1957).

Erik Erikson, a developmental psychologist, describes a similar process in his life span model. Erikson (1950/1963) writes of the "readiness" for each of eight subsequent developmental life tasks culminating in the final life tasks of generativity and integrity. Each progressive task or stage is not so much a cognitive process requiring moral will, but rather involves affects or feelings in the psychological "readiness" for the task. The central task in his life span model is generativity—the care and nurturing of the next generation (Westermeyer, 2004; Vaillant 2002, 2012).

Gandhi's notion of joy in social activism is similar to Erikson's affective readiness for each developmental life task. Rather than being a chore, when one is ready for generativity in such life tasks as parenting or mentoring, it is easily and naturally done for others out of a desire to do so. It can't be faked. Social activism from this perspective is not a burden or moral obligation done out of feelings of guilt or shame—it is a joy to do.

Empirically, generativity and other forms of social activism are associated with mental health and various metrics of positive functioning (Westermeyer, 2004, 2013; Vaillant, 2002). The focus on others rather than an excessive focus on the self may diminish anxiety and depression. From another perspective, severe symptoms may disrupt one's capacity for altruism or empathy. In any case, joy is associated with authentic care for others.

Am I suggesting that hugging abandoned or neglected children who are desperate to be hugged and loved is an act of social justice? Yes, I think so. The road to living and loving well, as Gandhi (1957) suggests, is finding and developing that joy in whatever altruistic service or loving relationship you choose. Perhaps one may be more likely to experience Campbell's all-too-rare epiphanies in the process.

Not easily done, I would guess, but for a moment in my life, in that church, it was a radiant experience to be treasured and not forgotten.

# CHAPTER 6
## THE CHOICE

························································

"Healthy children will not fear life if their elders have integrity enough not to fear death."

- Erik Erikson, *Childhood and Society*, 1950/1963

"I've lost a lot of friends as well as my parents. A realization has come to me very, very keenly, however, that I haven't lost them. That moment that I was with them has an everlasting quality about it that is now still with me. What it gave me then is still with me, and there's a kind of intimation of immortality in that."- Joseph Campbell, *The Power of Myth with Bill Moyers*, 1991

Mike Jenkins often visits Hospital Divina Providencia, one of the few hospices in Central America. The staff know him well, and I have accompanied him there many times. He visits the patients and distributes words of kindness along with photographs he has taken of them, writing materials, chocolates, and other gifts. The hospice residents sometimes do not have photographs or written material to leave relatives upon their death.

Sister Julia is the chief administrator of the hospice. We meet with her on virtually all of our visits. The Hospital Divina Providencia includes the former, meager, living quarters of Archbishop Saint Óscar Romero and the chapel where he was assassinated. A museum in his small, modest, living quarters contains photos, historical documents, and some of his humble possessions. Romero's living quarters suggest that he insisted on living as the poor lived, simply and unpretentiously. Sister Julia personally knew the archbishop and spoke fondly in remembrance of him to us.

The hospice patients are of all ages, from young children to the elderly. Most have terminal cancer of various types. Virtually all of them cannot afford medical treatment. Consequently, there is a waiting list to enter the hospice, which subsidizes their care. Some family members visit their relatives daily. There are financial issues regarding visitations because relatives sometimes cannot afford transportation costs, food, or other living expenses to visit the hospice if they have long distances to travel. Mike set up a transportation fund to enable relatives to visit patients at the hospice.

Another major issue for the hospice is the cost of medications. Medications to relieve suffering, such as morphine, are in short supply. Patients sometimes go without pain relief. This is a major problem worldwide for people living in extreme or moderate poverty. Not only do they suffer from higher rates of mortality and morbidity than those better off financially, but they also face a higher probability of excruciating, prolonged pain with death.

One day, we visited several patients, including Regina. She was a dignified looking woman who appeared to be about 50 years old. Her daughter was with her constantly. When Mike asked if she needed anything, Regina joked that she could use some chocolate. Mike laughed and gave her some that he had brought along for patients. I was struck by her dignity, serenity, and good humor in the face of death.

On returning to the hospice a few days later, we found that Regina had died within the hour and spent some time with her. I am always profoundly affected by the humanity of hospice patients facing death and understand why Mike repeatedly returns to visit them. In the most difficult circumstances that human beings find themselves, one often finds the best of human nature.

Over the years, Mike has maintained contact with a few of the family members of patients who have died at the hospice. As Erikson's (1950/1963) quote above suggests, endings are always about beginnings as well. Hospice visitations create lasting memories among family members and friends for the remainder of their lives.

Those we love who have died continue to live inside us (Vaillant, 1993). It is a theme mentioned by many psychologists of different theoretical orientations. They live in our memories of them; in the love they gave us and the love we have for them; in their values and ideals that we choose to emulate; and in the kindnesses we show to others as an extension of the kindnesses they showed to us. They become part of us, and we impart part of them to future generations.

Mike, John, and I became good friends at the hospice with

Lydia, who died at age 28 of cancer. We continued to visit Lydia's two young daughters over a 9-year period at their home in the mountains of north-central El Salvador. The two sisters, Esmeralda and Jacki, lived with their grandmother, Señora Toni. We watched them grow from childhood to their late teenage years. Jacki overcame a severe yearlong depression following her mother's death. We lost track of them due to the distance we had to travel to visit them. Esmeralda and Jacki have many photos to help keep the memory of their mother alive.

Mike has several poignant stories of individuals he has met over the years at the hospice. One story involves Faith, a 12-year-old girl, who was dying of leukemia. Mike did not see her for some time and assumed she died between his visits. Over a year later, however, Mike received a telephone call. The caller mentioned Faith. Mike, not recognizing the voice, responded that Faith had died at the hospice.

But the caller was Faith. Miraculously, her cancer spontaneously remitted and she was released from the hospice. Faith was now contacting her old friend, Mike. Out of hundreds of patients that Mike met at the hospice over the years, Faith was the only one to survive. In typical Mike fashion, he connected Faith with a donor in the United States who provided a scholarship for her to attend and graduate from both high school and college. Today, she is a mother and is working for the government. She has been cancer free for over 15 years.

## THE CHOICE

• • • • • • • • • • • • • • • • • •

Another memorable hospice narrative involves Jasmine, a 24-year-old woman. Soon after admission to the hospice with terminal cancer, it was discovered that Jasmine was expecting her first child.

The doctors presented Jasmine with a difficult choice. They could continue to treat her cancer with chemotherapy and thus prolong her life or perhaps cause the cancer to go into remission. Conversely, chemotherapy would likely take the life of her unborn child. In stark terms, Jasmine had to choose whether to have the baby and die without treatment or continue treatment with certain death for her unborn child.

Jasmine chose life for her infant and death for herself. This choice was not a certainty. There was a question about whether she would live long enough to be able to give birth and be far enough along in the pregnancy that her child would be sufficiently healthy to survive. Jasmine would give her life to ensure a greater possibility that her child would live. She expressed to all one final wish that was most important to her: to live long enough to hold her newborn child.

As the weeks unfolded, the people and routines of the hospice dramatically changed. The staff was transfixed with caring for Jasmine. Always a tight-knit and compassionate group in the face of working where the people they cared for and got to know intimately died, they suddenly faced the prospect of new life coming to the hospice. All were devoted to bringing that life into the world and ensuring that the newborn's life would continue after the mother died. The change in the outlook and activity of nurses, doctors, and other staff members was palpable. No effort was spared on Jasmine's behalf. Her condition and the health of the developing fetus were of utmost concern in their daily lives. Weeks turned into months as the pregnancy progressed.

Jasmine had a healthy baby boy, Carlos. Family and staff alike celebrated his birth. Jasmine got her wish and held her baby encircled by happy staff, friends, and family. Moreover, Jasmine enjoyed the company of her newborn son at the hospice for about a year before she succumbed to cancer.

Jasmine's sister and her husband raised Carlos after Jasmine's death. Mike stays in contact with this family. Carlos is now a healthy 10-year-old boy. He prizes a photograph of himself with his mother taken soon before her death in the hospice. This photo is prominently displayed in his home. (See this photo with others in the back of this book.)

# CHAPTER 7
## JORGE AND ERIKA: SIBLINGS

> "Sarah (my wife) was also impressed by the cohesion she saw in sibling groups in the villages of Nepal and south India and even more in rural Mexico. . . . She often heard from Mexican friends that in a fiercely competitive world they could only count on the support of close kin—and of siblings in particular." - LeVine & LeVine, *Do Parents Matter*, 2016

The above observation by Robert and Sarah LeVine, prominent anthropologists/psychologists, also applies well to siblings in El Salvador and especially to Jorge and Erika. Time and time again, the power of family relationships, and of sibling relations in particular, is a strong bond supporting our students through traumatic or stressful events. Saint Romero in his radio broadcasts on Sundays to the people usually referred to them as "brothers and sisters."

Jorge is 3 years older than his sister, Erika. They have one older brother, José. Their parents, Silvio and Lola, had little education. Lola was from a large family. She completed seventh grade but was not able to continue in school. Lola worked part time as a seamstress. Silvio was also from a large family and was never able to attend school. He usually worked farming a small plot of land, but sometimes worked in construction, if work was available. Early in Jorge's life, the family lived in his paternal grandmother's house, which was made of dried palm trees, sticks, and plastics. It had a dirt floor.

An earthquake in 2001 forced the family to move to an even poorer community, which was arranged for 100 families in the earthquake region who had lost their homes. Life in this community was difficult. The family had to carry drinking water to their home from wells located some distance away. A river separated the area from other communities. As there were no bridges, people had to wade across the river to enter or leave the community.

For their first few years, Silvio and Lola had to carry Jorge and José across the river on their backs twice a day to get them to and from school. During stretches of the rainy season, the river could not be forded and no one entered or left the community. After some years had passed, the community received donations to provide better sources of drinking water and to build a bridge across the river.

Silvio periodically gained part-time work in construction, which temporarily helped the financial fortunes of the family. He also worked as a tenant farmer. Children typically contribute to the economic productivity of households throughout the developing world. Thus, his two sons, and eventually his daughter, worked in the fields when they were not in school. During times of strained economic conditions, the children had to work full time and could not attend school.

Throughout grade school and high school, Jorge earned

outstanding grades. He was a straight A student in high school and graduated as the valedictorian of his class. Due to his excellent academic record, Jorge received a Project Salvador scholarship to the university.

The scholarship program usually gave preference to women rather than men. Tony Gasbarro, the program's founder, and others (including Melinda Gates) recognized that education for women often has more of a positive impact on needy communities than education for men. Families and communities more often prize the value of education through the efforts of a mother, who bears the primary responsibility for raising children and being responsible for protecting, nurturing, and educating the next generation. The education of women powerfully advances families and communities (Gates, 2019; LeVine & LeVine, 2016).

Boys and men, however, also benefit from an education. They are at special risk for gang recruitment in El Salvador. Gangs provide a group identity, a job, and a supporting, protecting organization for them (Wolfe, 2017). Similarly, an education provides them an identity, a potential career, and financial support. Thus, education is a crucial alternative to entering gang life or a way out of the gang culture.

José did not continue with his education after high school because the family could not afford it. Despite grades as good as or better than his brother and later his sister, he started working to help support the family.

Jorge was particularly qualified to succeed in the university. In addition to his excellent academic credentials, from a young age Jorge demonstrated a burning desire to attain a professional career. Jorge chose to study mathematics, an especially rigorous subject that he loved, and planned to be a mathematics teacher. He spent his spare time voluntarily tutoring children and adults in mathematics.

Jorge displayed a kind, gentle, and somewhat shy demeanor with us. However, he could be firm and at times showed great courage to rebuff gang attempts to recruit him. For some reason, the gangs left him alone, although danger was often present.

Jorge achieved success in college beyond expectations. Succeeding at the university was formidable in Jorge's mathematics program. Some professors could be unreasonably difficult with students. The initial cohort of 85 mathematics students was significantly reduced over the first 2 years. Nevertheless, Jorge received nearly straight A grades and professors selected him to be a teaching assistant. Jorge also volunteered to tutor other students in his community.

Meanwhile, Erika finished high school with outstanding grades as well. She dreamed of a professional career in engineering by which she could develop the exceptional talent that she knew she possessed. But Silvio maintained that he could not support both of his children at the university, and if one goes to study the other cannot. Erika was devastated by this news. She became depressed with the reality that she would not be able to attend the university and realize her dream. She went to her room and cried continually in despair. Her parents and brothers reached out to console her and help her accept economic reality. Erika could not be consoled.

Jorge decided to request help for his sister. Although naturally reserved, he met with Beto and John on one of our visits, which was about the time Erika was told she could not continue her education. As his talented younger sister was finishing high school and needing a scholarship to the university, Jorge requested of us a scholarship for her.

An informal policy of the scholarship program was to limit one scholarship to a single family at one time to spread the possibilities of an education across several families. However, Erika's academic record was as good as—and perhaps better than—Jorge's record. Moreover, Jorge's request was poignant. He advocated for his sister whom he loved dearly.

The group visiting El Salvador that summer could not refuse Jorge's request for his sister, especially a sister so qualified. The seven of us took a personal collection that would pay the $1,200 scholarship fund for Erika's first year. The plan then was to include Erika as an official scholarship student in her second year at the university. It was uncharacteristic of Jorge to assert himself in requesting help for his sister. But we understood the love he felt as they walked home with his arm on her shoulder, giving her the news of her opportunity for an education.

Erika wanted to study electrical engineering—not a traditional subject for a young woman in El Salvador. She was one of only three women in the university's electrical engineering program. Similar to Jorge, Erika possesses a quiet, studious, respectful demeanor. She turned out to be an absolute success at the university. Erika is a straight A student, besting most of her peers in her rigorous program. She receives rave reviews from her professors.

For the last 2 years of Jorge's college education, he traveled to and from the university with Erika. They encouraged each other and helped each other study. In the mornings, they labored with their father in the farm fields to better support the family financially. Then they studied the rest of the day.

Soon after Erika started at the university, Jorge received a threat of physical harm through social media. The threat read: "How do you want to die, as an ant or a rodent? A rodent dies alone, and if you choose to die as an ant dies, your whole family will be killed." The family believed the threat came from unknown individuals in the community who envied the fact that two members from the same, impoverished family were attending the university and may eventually achieve a professional status and income.

The family did not know the credibility of the threat, which caused great anxiety. But Jorge and Erika were undeterred from continuing their studies. They were determined to succeed. Although nothing came of the threat, the incident indicates that students may have to cope with threats and jealousy in the community. There may be unforeseen perils in attempting to succeed.

Jorge graduated from college with honors in a mathematics specialty. John and I attended his graduation and the happy celebration afterward with the family at a local restaurant. Jorge was one of only six in mathematics out of an initial class of 85 students to graduate on schedule. He is now looking for employment while he takes English lessons. The ability to speak English would significantly improve his career opportunities since many businesses require English-speaking skills in the country.

Although Jorge has had to overcome much adversity, he is filled with gratitude for what he has had rather than regrets for what he does not have. Jorge commented in a written statement as follows:

> If I had the opportunity to be born again, I would prefer to be born in the same conditions. Everything I have lived has been very special. It has taught me to value life, to value how little I have and how much I have achieved. It has taught me to value my family, friends, and the environment in which I grew up. . . I thank all of my friends who gave me the opportunity to meet them and give me their friendship. That made my university life a fun place which I will never forget since it will be marked forever in my heart.

Gratitude is a marker of mental health and maturity (Vaillant, 2002, 2012). It is a remarkable healing and coping force.

Jorge and Erika also have gratitude and love for their older brother, José, who left school after high school, has a job, and lives with the family with his common-law wife, Melia. Melia gave birth to their first child recently, bringing joy to the whole family.

José has a grossly disfiguring and large birthmark that covers most of his face and neck. The birthmark resembles a large tattoo that gang members sometimes have on their faces to identify themselves as gang members and to intimidate others. This distinguishing birthmark dramatically alters his life. He fears—and there is reason for this fear—that his birthmark will identify him as a gang member to the larger world. If gangs identify him as a rival gang member, he would be in danger. He further fears that police authorities will also identify him as a gang member, which would increase the possibility of extrajudicial police actions against him.

Given these realistic risks, José frequently isolates himself at home for fear of discrimination or violent attacks. He sometimes identifies himself as a pariah among his fellow human beings and assumes others find him physically unacceptable. José has inquired about the possibility of cosmetic facial operations to remove the birthmark. Such operations, however, are financially prohibitive given the current meager family financial resources and the exorbitant costs of the operations. José also was a good student in high school and hopes eventually to enter the university.

Erika and Jorge worry about their brother who they know to be a different person than what others sometimes interpret based on his birthmark. A strong sibling bond suggests that Jorge and Erika will support José throughout his life. They plan to financially help their brother through school when they start earning money. They know him beyond the face he presents to the public.

I have seen remarkable changes in both Jorge and Erika over the years as they develop as scholars in their chosen careers. It is also noteworthy to understand the changes in their father at the same time.

Silvio raised his family through difficult, physical labor, typically earning between $5 and $10 per day when he was able to find work. Curiously, this man with three academically gifted children is unable to read or write as he never attended school. Others helped him understand the menu at the restaurant where we celebrated Jorge's graduation.

Despite the absence of an education, Silvio is a man of great integrity, dignity, and values. He credits his father, also a subsistence farmer, with teaching him to always do the "correct" thing. Although so many of the young people we encounter have been abandoned by their fathers, Silvio is committed and loyal to his family. Jorge maintains that his father made "thousands" of sacrifices over more than 2 decades to financially support and mentor his children.

Silvio taught his children the values of honesty, integrity, and hard work that he learned from his parents. The lesson for me in observing this family is that some things are more important than education in raising a family. Wisdom, integrity, and love transcend wealth and education. Silvio and Lola imparted love and a committed morality to their children that made a fertile terrain for their subsequent education and growth. In turn, José, Jorge, and Erika are grateful to their parents for "thousands" of sacrifices on their behalf.

Silvio had reservations about his children getting an education. Initially, he was opposed to Jorge attending college. He particularly had doubts about Erika going to the university because he did not think it was necessary for a woman to further her education to fulfill the traditional woman's role in his community. Typical of many cultures, investment for an education is more likely to be made for males than females across the developing world (Gates, 2019; LeVine, LeVine, Schnell-Anzola, Rowe & Dexter, 2012).

Silvio changed. He is now proud that Erika is getting an education and of the outstanding grades his children have earned. Jorge and Erika, incredibly talented siblings, now have the opportunity to achieve unimagined success given their humble background with no resources for a college education.

At Jorge's graduation ceremony, John and I observed that the president of the university, several administrators, and many professors are women. Moreover, many of the graduates are women, including the sole student speaker, the valedictorian of the class. The world is changing for the better.

Recently, John asked Jorge: "Who is smarter, you or Erika?" Jorge smiled and confessed that Erika is better in some areas of academics than he. But given the close, supportive relationships of siblings in El Salvador, he said it with pride, love, and goodwill. Sibling rivalry drains away in these families in which brothers and sisters rely closely on each other for support across the life span.

# CHAPTER 8
# HOPES AND DREAMS

••••••••••••••••••••••••••••••••••••••••••••••••••••••

"The death of self-esteem can occur quickly, easily in children, before their ego has 'legs' so to speak. Couple the vulnerability of youth with indifferent parents, dismissive adults, and a world, which in its language, laws and images, re-enforces despair, and the journey to destruction is sealed."

- Toni Morrison, *The Bluest Eye*, 1970/2007

"There are those that look at things the way they are and ask why? I dream of things that never were, and ask why not?"

- George Bernard Shaw, *Back to Methuselah*, act 1, 1921

In July a couple of years ago, John and I traveled to Sonsonate, a small city in northwest El Salvador, with Beto, Marisol, and other staff members. We visited several high school and college students in a monthly meeting that monitors their progress in the scholarship program. We planned to meet many new students in the program for the first time.

Most students enter the scholarship program at the beginning of high school. As we arrived at the site, there were eight mothers with their adolescent children waiting to request a scholarship for high school. Unfortunately, there are not enough scholarships for the many qualified and motivated students. Beto took the names of the students waiting for us with their mothers. He explained that they would be part of a list of students applying for scholarships if more funding becomes available.

Beto and the in-country staff also screen candidates for grades and financial need to select the best students for college. The college students are selected from the current group of high school students. A continuing major issue for the scholarship program is how best to assess high school students for college scholarships.

Meetings give John and me an opportunity to see which high school students may be a good fit for college scholarships. The best predictor of future success in any domain is a history of past success in that same domain. Consequently, the students' high school academic record is an important criterion for scrutinizing good candidates for college scholarships.

One of the high school students, Griselda, was noticeably more pro-active and confident than the other high school girls. I had heard about Griselda earlier from Beto. He wanted to give her a scholarship for college starting the following year based on her rare, outstanding grades. Griselda had near perfect A grades throughout high school.

All the high school girls, except for Griselda, spoke in Spanish. Much to my surprise, Griselda spoke to us in English. To learn English in her free time took a tremendous effort in addition to maintaining a high grade point average in her other high school subjects. Griselda spoke steadily and with much feeling. At 17 years of age, she exuded confidence and competence.

Beto asked each high student about their dreams for the future. Griselda stated that she dreamed of being an astronaut, a near impossibility for an impoverished girl from the country in El Salvador.

Dreams and hopes for the future say so much about one's cultural context and norms for achieving life goals. Disadvantaged or oppressed groups may have restricted hopes. Subtle social oppression may involve communicating to poor or discriminated groups, especially girls, that they do not have the ability to achieve success in certain occupations. Oppressive social expectations may dictate that they should not even aspire for success or an education.

Covert and subconscious oppression may be destructive to striving for a better life. It may involve a pernicious process of self-stigmatization in that persons absorb negative social messages that a group may be defective in some way. This self-stigma may become part of one's identity, which may prohibit an individual from hoping or trying to achieve higher goals.

Success becomes feared because it does not fit a preordained self-identity or the traditions of one's family history or culture. Success in these circumstances is sometimes unconsciously connected to destruction for one not deserving of success. Thus, a destructive self-stigmatizing process may stop disadvantaged people from striving for an education. All of the scholarship students in our program (except for siblings in the program) are the first in their families to attend college or, in many cases, high school. They do not have models for educational achievements.

In the mental health field, investigators describe the pernicious effects of self-stigma on the severely mentally ill in seeking help and achieving recovery (Corrigan, Druss & Perlick, 2014). Moreover, Voisin (2019) discusses the restricted life goals of young, African American men living in violent, marginal communities in Chicago.

Miranda, one of the scholarship students, was not supported by her parents in her quest for a scholarship and an education. When her older brother left home to live with his girlfriend and her older sister had a baby, Miranda was expected by the family to do more chores and devote less time to her education. Her parents disparaged her abilities and discouraged her desire for an education. When Miranda attained the college scholarship, her mother told her: "So what? You will drop out or flunk out anyway."

On another occasion when Miranda was studying late into the night, her father told her to "shut off the light and stop wasting electricity." He indicated that her education was not worth her effort. Miranda responded to her father, a minister: "How can you treat me like this and still be true to the fact that you are a pastor?"

Miranda considered leaving home to live somewhere else with her boyfriend but was convinced to stay in her home by the staff.

Miranda turned out to be an outstanding student, receiving nearly a straight A average in her chosen field of study, mathematics, and is now in her third year of study in a 5-year program. She plans to go on after college to attain a master's degree in mathematics. Miranda is determined to be a college teacher. Despite negative messages from her parents, she retains within herself a self-respect as well as extraordinary talent that drives her academic achievement. She perseveres in her studies.

Miranda's face lit up when we acknowledged her and her good grades, and told her that we "believe in you." We told her that we are committed to her completing her education and that she would not be abandoned.

Gates (2019) writes about how low self-image is a key feature that may prohibit achievement for young women throughout the world. Gates sees education as crucial in changing a low self-image in societies where women are second-class citizens. Gates (2019) writes:

> All the women I've talked to and all the data I've seen convince me that the most transforming force of education for women and girls is changing the self-image of girls who go to school. . . That is the secret of an empowering education: A girl learns she is not who she's been told she is. She is the equal of anyone, and she has rights she needs to assert and defend. This is how the great movements of social change get traction: when outsiders reject the low self-image society has imposed on them and begin to author a self-image of their own.

Miranda's plans to become a university professor and Griselda's hopes for herself to become an astronaut transcended their gender and place in society. Unlike many other disadvantaged young women the world over, Miranda and Griselda aimed high. Their hopes as well as their outstanding grades mark them as extraordinary.

Griselda allowed herself a goal of being an astronaut. Her good grades belied this dream as mere fantasy. Miranda would not be deterred by disparaging remarks that devalued the ability she knows she possesses.

Our lives may be restricted in subtle or unconscious ways by a programmed, culturally sanctioned script of limited goals. For some reason, Griselda and Miranda would have none of it.

I thought it was not so important to ultimately achieve adolescent dreams for oneself. Rather, to dream and believe one can succeed is most important. Indeed, a year later Griselda reported that she now wanted to be a geophysicist and study the actions of volcanoes, a much-needed profession in El Salvador, which is sometimes known as the land of volcanos. Today, she is studying geophysical sciences at the university. As expected, her first-year university grades were excellent. Her academic performance in a rigorous program justifies her high goals for herself. Griselda is confident that she can succeed.

To hope to rise as far as one's imagination and ability can take one and to set goals for that end indicate a certain level of self-respect and self-esteem. The dreams of impoverished youth need to be encouraged to help them persevere in the face of so much adversity.

As a teacher, I feel that one of the worst mistakes I could make with students was to discourage them from some life goal or dream or imply that they are not capable of learning. Accordingly, my critique of their work must be done with utmost care and specificity. If they are doing unfavorably in my class, I specify what actions they need to take to succeed and perhaps refer them for writing remediation or other support. Moreover, I emphasize they can improve and succeed with remediation and effort. Comments condemning them to a sense of some personal contamination that cannot be corrected is destructive to their self-confidence and future efforts. The psychological component of education involves encouragement and inspiration to help students overcome phobias or destructive self-images.

As the young women spoke at the meeting, I noticed a marked difference supporting Gates' (2019) observations that education can make all the difference in one's self-image. Each young woman in succession around the group had an opportunity to speak. The high school students in the meeting were generally quiet and shy in comparison to the college students. They had little to say and seemed frightened to speak, to stand out in any way, or to ask us questions.

In contrast, the college women were talkative and confident. Certainly, age and various experiences play a role in this transformation. One can observe such differences in virtually any society comparing high school students to college students. Nevertheless, I thought that education made the college students more motivated and confident in comparison to peers who had not gone to college.

Moreover, I observed the college students in the scholarship program longitudinally over many years. They had career goals for themselves that they were achieving step by step. Education empowered them to hope and see opportunities they could achieve through their own effort and abilities. The women spoke longer, with better eye contact, and with more feeling and self-assurance.

These young women found their voices with an education. Of course, I observe the same transformation among my students at Adler University from their first-year classes with me in graduate school, to my work with them on dissertations just prior to graduation, and finally to follow-ups with alumni in productive careers 5, 10, and 20 years later. They frequently surpass the knowledge and skills of their former teachers. Nevertheless, the similar process of growth among impoverished girls in El Salvador has been more remarkable to observe because the initial, negative, self-stigmatizing bias may be greater than more privileged groups.

The college group at the meeting that day included Diana, an outgoing, spirited, young woman of about 21 years. She is studying languages at the university and hopes to work as a teacher or translator for the Salvadoran government. Diana said the scholarship changed her life, and when she graduates she hopes to change others' lives for the better. After our interview with Diana, she came up to us and asked if we remembered her name. When we apologized, she responded, "My name is Diana. I want you always to please remember my name." Subsequently, we have always remembered Diana's name.

Diana studied English at the university. She translated for other students from Spanish to English for part of the meeting. Diana is bright, inquisitive, and assertive in a healthy way. She exudes a positive self-respect. She spoke up at several points in the meeting and later at lunch to ask questions or to make comments.

We later heard a story about Diana regarding another university student and her close friend, Inez, age 23. Inez was verbally harassed in a sexual manner by a teacher in class. Diana is a member of the student council, which has a great deal of influence at the university. When Diana learned that the professor was harassing her good friend, she gave Inez a T-shirt that council members wear to identify themselves. Diana told Inez to wear the T-shirt to the professor's class and to sit in the front row.

The covert message was that Inez belonged to the student council, an organization that proactively advocates for students and that can file complaints regarding inappropriate or harassing behavior from teachers if need be. The teacher could be scrutinized by the student council and others. The harassment stopped in his class. Diana has guts. She is loyal and supportive of her fellow students. As a student leader, she is ready to take action to address grievances.

John and I observe the miracle of education for many young women in El Salvador. With time and experience, they become aware of their abilities. They proactively develop skills in their respective professions. Most importantly, their self-image evolves to greater self-respect and dignity to support lofty dreams for themselves.

# CHAPTER 9
# MORE STUDENT STORIES

..............................................................

"I don't read and write, but now my daughter can read and write. So now I feel like I can read and write as well."

- Mother of a student in the scholarship program

"The study of child development has been largely confined to children in North America, Europe and other Western countries, who comprise less than 10 percent of all children in the world. . . .

"The more professional experts on child rearing propagated universal concepts of the normal child, the clearer it became to anthropologists that the concepts were fashioned from local (that is, Euroamerican or Western) moral standards combined with biological speculation."

- Robert A. LeVine and Rebecca S. New,
*Anthropology and Child Development*, 2008

A cross-cultural perspective, as Robert LeVine and Rebecca New (2008) suggest, means being open, in a nonjudgmental fashion, to the adaptive possibilities of cultural norms that differ from what we have experienced or have been taught in our society, which comprises a small minority of the world's people. Cross-cultural study reveals to us the diversity of the human experience and that various cultural norms and practices different from our own do not result in psychopathology or abnormality but rather adaptation to the ecological niche of that society. The following are some brief life histories of other college students in the scholarship program that illustrate cross-cultural diversity and adaptation.

## SUSAN

•••••••••••••••••

Susan was in the scholarship program for 7 years before graduating with a law degree a few years ago. Her father abandoned the family when she was a little girl and did not support Susan growing up. Susan lives with her mother, Marta, and several siblings in a village in El Salvador. Marta worked in the mayor's office in town and was extremely supportive of Susan's education. While Marta was only able to finish the fourth grade, she was determined to help Susan succeed.

Marta, along with other mothers, hosted many lunches for us over the years in her home. She shared that her daughter was happy studying at the university, and as long as her daughter was happy, she was happy. It is always inspiring to witness the extensive parental commitment to the education of their children. They place their hopes in education so their children will have a better life than they have had.

Susan is sociable and always smiling. She is close to and supportive of her younger siblings, especially Daniel who is about 13 years younger than Susan. Susan brought Daniel to every meeting that we have with the students—without exception. Daniel hopes to follow his older sister into the scholarship program. Like his sister, Daniel aspires to be an attorney.

After graduation, Susan continued to bring Daniel to every meeting. We asked students and alumni of the scholarship program to speak to the group about their progress in education or in life after graduation. Susan is always a willing speaker. She is articulate as well as politically and socially skilled in her interactions with others. Before graduating, Susan worked temporarily for a judge. After graduation from law school, she was able to get a six-month job that paid well and involved voter registration.

Although for some periods after graduation Susan was unemployed, she was never upset or depressed. Rather, in a talk she gave she expressed how grateful she was for her education and the temporary jobs. I am, however, continually concerned about the job prospects of each student following graduation. Job opportunity is a major economic issue in El Salvador, which has a high unemployment rate. Within the last two years, officials from a local political party approached Susan about running for vice mayor of her municipality. Susan believed it was because she had a law degree and was one of only five individuals who have a college degree in her village. Her education positioned her for job opportunities.

Susan agreed to be a candidate and won the election for a 3-year term. She now officiates at civil marriage ceremonies, administers a fund to help local indigent people, and manages many other government functions at city hall. Susan is bright, qualified, and learns quickly.

She is setting up her own private law practice in her community and intends to specialize in women's issues. Susan recently passed an exam for a Notary Certificate, which is a major accomplishment that will greatly enhance her earning prospects. With her new job and an increase in income, Susan was been able to move her family into a new house.

Susan has married 50 couples as part of her job at city hall. She is developing a range of administrative and political skills. Susan now speaks with greater authority to community groups. This once disadvantaged girl has blossomed into a political pillar of her community in Lincoln-like fashion.

Susan commented on the scholarship program:

> The program has changed my life. I never thought growing up that I would become an attorney and help my family as I have been able to do. Thanks to God for having placed in my path people who have helped me so much in my life. The scholarship program has helped me not only to achieve a degree, but it has supported me emotionally and as a person.

## ROSITA, CRUZ, AND FAMILY

·················

Rosita and Cruz (introduced in Chapter 1) were two of our scholarship students. They are two of five sisters raised by their mother who earned a minimum wage by selling fruit in an open market. Their mother scraped by on subsistence level work to provide for her five daughters and herself. Their father abandoned the family many years ago. Rosita and Cruz were the first in their extended family to graduate from college. Rosita works as a high school teacher. Cruz recently graduated in accounting and is working for a private company.

Several years ago at one of the monthly meetings, Cruz started to speak but then broke down in tears while describing a recent incident. The family returned to their home to find it empty—with all their belongings taken from them. After inquiring about the theft with neighbors, their belongings returned anonymously. A few days later, three men with guns appeared on their property. The men told the family that they liked the house in which the family was living and would like to move into the house.

The intimidating actions of these street gang members frightened the women. Gangs sometimes take over buildings in a similar fashion to establish a presence in the community. They intimidate households into abandoning homes and buildings with the threat of violence.

For example, about five years ago, another scholarship student, Patricia, lived in a small farming community in a remote region of the country when several armed gang members showed up at her door. They demanded $10,000 in extortion money to be paid by the next morning. Patricia's family was to collect the money from other households in the community or one member of her family would be killed the next day. Unable to pay such a large amount of money, the family left their home that night in their old pickup truck and never returned to the area. The gang then seized their house and the surrounding property.

Rosita, Cruz, and their family had nowhere else to go. Moreover, there was no one in authority from whom to request help. They decided to stay in their home despite the threat and set up a schedule so someone was always in the house with the door locked. They lived in constant fear that the gang members would return.

They reasoned that they may have been chosen because of the isolated location of their home (it is down a long path without access to a street) or the fact that there were no men in their household. Regardless of the reason, the family was traumatized by the threat.

Days, weeks, and months went by without incident. Slowly, the women felt less anxious about the gang members returning. With more income from Rosita and Cruz, they renovated their home and still live there today.

Similar incidents of intimidation occur daily in various ways in gang territories throughout Honduras, Guatemala, and El Salvador.

## DIEGO

•••••••••••••••••••

Diego is a 22-year-old who recently graduated as an agronomist from the university. He is bright and worked hard in an academically difficult program. Carmen, Beto Rivera's mother-in-law who regularly participates in mentoring the scholarship students, convinced Diego to enter a scholastically rigorous program that, if successful, would more likely result in a rewarding and lucrative career. As Carmen predicted, Diego gained part-time employment in his chosen profession prior to graduation.

Diego's father abandoned his family many years ago for work in the United States. As a single parent, his mother struggled to keep the family together. Diego debated whether to attend the university or forgo an education and start working at age 18 to support the family. His mother, however, encouraged Diego to study at the university rather than seek employment.

Diego was persistent in achieving an education despite not having a paternal role model growing up and struggling with issues of financial resources. He worries about being able to obtain full-time employment after graduation. He is currently looking for a job. He has a steady girlfriend whom he would like to marry and start a family. Diego is concerned about being accepted by his girlfriend's father, who has reservations about a disadvantaged young man from the campo.

In one meeting with us, Diego commented that, unlike other scholarship students at the university, he personally meets with his benefactors. Apparently, this has made a difference to Diego and other scholarship students. If others whom they personally meet believe in them, Diego concludes, they are more likely to find in themselves the strength to persist and be successful.

## ALICIA

...................

Alicia is a 23-year-old woman who graduated from college with a degree in business administration and accounting. Soon after graduating, she married her best friend, Rodney.

Alicia's mother needed a major operation. The family raised funds by borrowing money and requesting donations from friends and their extended family. This is a typical strategy in El Salvador for surgery or necessary medical care. Over 76% of Salvadorans do not have medical insurance (Wolfe, 2017).

The family lives in a dangerous neighborhood bordering two gang territories. Alicia's father works as a laborer for low pay. He has been extorted, tortured, and beaten by gang members twice when traveling to work. In addition, Alicia had a gun put to her head on her way home, and the assailant demanded that she go with him. When observing Alicia's brother waiting for her at a distance, the assailant left the scene. To better ensure her physical safety, Alicia periodically shares a residence with friends near the university to avoid risky travel to and from her parents' home.

Despite such trauma and family financial issues, Alicia has a ready smile and is always affable with everyone she meets. After much sacrifice and hard work, she happily graduated from college and married Rodney. She is putting together a budget and raising capital to open a restaurant near the university.

Alicia commented recently:

> I am so very grateful to God and to all of those people and to my sponsors who have contributed to my professional growth. I entered the scholarship program in 2009 and graduated in 2018. Without a doubt it has been wonderful to become a professional. In the future, I hope to own my own business, to bring employment to more young people, and to help sponsor scholarships for others. In this way, I can demonstrate my gratitude to those who have helped me realize my dream.

## LORETTA

·················

Loretta is a 25-year-old woman who graduated from college with a marketing degree. Her brother, Ricki, studies at the university and is part of the scholarship program. Her mother works as a housekeeper to support the family. Beto's brother-in-law, Rolando, hired Loretta in his business to give her a start in her career.

In gratitude Loretta stated:

> I have been in the scholarship program for 7 years, from my second year in high school until I graduated. My experiences have been an example to my siblings, who are fighting to achieve their dreams too. I want to give a special thanks to

my mother for all of the help and support that she has given to me throughout my life. Due to a lack of economic resources, she did not have the chance to continue in school. But her dream was always for her children to go to school and continue past grammar school. Now, I have received a university degree. My mother says that all the people who have given to the scholarship program are so special to us and will live in our hearts for the rest of our lives.

## CARI

...................

Cari is a 23-year old, single parent who gave birth to her son while she was in high school. The birth of her son made it difficult for her to continue her education. However, Cari, an excellent student, persevered in her studies. She is now in her third year at the university and is studying to be a primary school teacher. She loves to write poetry in her spare time. Cari lives with her father, two younger brothers, and a grandmother, who cares for her child while she attends the university. Cari commented as follows:

> I think that education is a fundamental pillar for the development of a country. In a few years, I will be contributing to such development by being a teacher myself. I will be a guardian of this pillar and would not be able to do this without the scholarship. The program has enabled me to grow as a person. I can only say that I am very grateful and that I am going to give the best of myself at every moment.

# CHAPTER 10
# STUDENTS SPEAK

······················································

"I have decided to travel... On this journey, I went through the revolutionary poetry of Roque Dalton, some of the Salvadoran narrative with Salarrué, the Universidad Nacional Autónoma de México with Roberto Bolano, and finally I got to know England with Jane Austen...

"I remember the best of these journeys. There are no boundaries or limits, just as the kindness and love of some people... I feel... happiness that many of us are making our dream come true thanks to those who decided to build this project to change lives and a whole nation, people to whom there are no boundaries or limits. Our journey never ends."

- Cari, a scholarship student

The students were asked to write statements about themselves and whatever they wished to say to donors of the scholarship programs in the United States. The following are some of their statements.

Diana, University Student (see Chapter 8)

•••••••••••••••••••

I wish a bunch of blessings for the people who have helped my dreams come true. My name is Diana. I am studying to become an English teacher. I live with my three siblings, my father, and my mother. My biggest dream is to finish my major successfully and help others with their dreams too. For example, I would like to give others a scholarship like the one I have now. Since this scholarship has changed my life, I would like to change other peoples' lives.

This scholarship has changed me economically and also morally. I feel really happy and capable when staff and other supporters tell me that they are proud of me. That encourages me to keep going and to be a better person and a better student.

As any young girl, I have lots of dreams. I would like to get a scholarship to earn a master's degree in translation. I would like to study and travel abroad, help my parents, and continue studying different languages. I would like to work as a translator in the embassy of my country and would like to work as a teacher. I would really like to share my knowledge with others. I think our society could change if we change and if we help others change their bad thoughts into good ones.

Finally, I would like to thank all of you for your donations. You are helping to change peoples' lives. You are changing countries. Although it would seem impossible, you are changing the world.

## Nicholas, University Student

•••••••••••••••••

My name is Nicholas, and I am in my first year at the university studying agro-industrial engineering. My life was difficult in childhood because my father died when I was 4 years old. For that reason, my mother took the role of mother and father at the same time. With great effort, she gave me the opportunity to study English in high school.

Thanks to God for this scholarship and an opportunity to improve my life. Thanks to all of the people who support this program. You are a special kind of people who believe in our capacity to improve and develop our country. We cannot repay the donation, but we have a way to show you how to help others.

## Miguel, University Student

•••••••••••••••••

I am studying to be a public accountant. I belong to a family in which there are myself, four younger children, and my mother. My mother had very few financial resources, and she could not afford to send me to school. For me, the scholarship program is not only support economically but morally as well.

My mother takes care of our house, and her name is Arlena. She studied until the fifth grade and has been an example to me. Whenever I am sad or depressed, she is the one person who inspires me and says, "Son, continue forward. This is only a small test for you that you will overcome. Remember that you have your siblings, and you have to be an example for them."

Erika, Electrical Engineering Student (See Chapter 7)

....................

I am a person of few resources. Thank you for believing in all of the scholarship students and for being a part of our lives. I will work very hard every day to be a better person and to merit the faith that you have in me. In that way, I can give you thanks for all that you are doing for me.

Esmeralda, Psychology Student

....................

I always give thanks first to God for placing people in my life who have helped me so much. The staff has helped me not only economically but emotionally. They always are asking us about our studies and our families. They ask about what concerns us and what we like. They are people who are very interested in us as persons. Thank you for all of the support that you are giving me.

Tatiana, High School Student

....................

I want to continue on to the university. I want to study medicine and become a pediatrician. I would like to help children who need help.

If I do have success in my career, I would like to give part of my money to a foundation that helps children with cancer. My interest in medicine began when I was 7 years old and lived in an institution, a place where many people lived together. I would see so many sick children there whose mothers could not take them to a doctor because they had no money. From that day on I told myself that I would become a doctor to help those people who most need helping.

For me, the scholarship program is a blessing. It is a program that most helps those who need assistance to stay in school. For me, it has been a huge help not only for the economic aid but also because those who run the program know how to motivate each of us and recognize our efforts. The program gives each of us an opportunity. I am so grateful for this opportunity to grow as a person and to be able to achieve my dreams.

Mercedes, High School Student

• • • • • • • • • • • • • • • • •

I am a student in my first year of high school. When I was told I was going to receive a scholarship, I really could not believe it. My father is a police officer and a large part of his salary is used to pay for the loan that allowed us to purchase a very small and humble house that we call our home. My family is small. I live with my father and mother and 11-year-old sister. My mother does not work and she and my father made the decision that it was better for my mother to stay at home taking care of me and my sister rather than taking the risk of leaving us alone given the situation in our country and the risk that my father runs every day in his work as a police officer. When my mother worked in a factory which made clothes, her pay was very low and did not allow enough money to pay for someone to take care of my sister and me.

With this opportunity that you have given me, I will study and do everything to better myself financially so that I can give my family a better way of life. Also, I do not want my country to continue the way it is and I want to contribute to the betterment of my country and other people that are in situations similar to mine. My father's salary is used to buy food and does not allow us to have luxuries in our home or to buy special clothes. My parents could not have purchased school supplies for me.

I will tell you that my parents believe that only through an education can I better myself. My ultimate goal is to help people with their problems and I would like to work with children. In the last year I had the opportunity to work with children in my church and I learned about the emotional problems that children may have. I want to be part of the solution to these problems in order that my country can better itself.

I give you many, many thanks for this opportunity. I commit myself to doing everything with all of my heart to take advantage of this opportunity. I hope that God multiplies your blessings a thousand times for the help that you have given each one of the scholarship recipients even though you have never met us.

## Karen, Business Administration Student

••••••••••••••••

I live with my parents and two sisters. They have always supported me and encouraged me to continue and complete my studies. When I am not studying, I work with an association that helps military veterans and another organization that works to find ways to help poor people. Thank you for the help and support with which you have blessed me—not only for economic support but for the workshops, which have enabled me to become a better person.

## Cari, Education Student (See Chapter 9)

••••••••••••••••

From the patio of my home, I am able to observe so many stars. It appears that there is a battle among them.

I ask myself if the light from these stars is like the light from a person who fights against adversity, who fights each day to be a better person, who follows a clear path to fulfill his or her dreams, who helps the next person without expecting anything in return. I think that both light up the world.

The cold makes the night its own, and I think of the family that is in my heart. Yes, those of us who are not united biologically but who are united through our hearts, this family through which we discover a new world in which being ourselves is a great treasure, which sees and helps us grow . . . my second family, the family of the scholarship program.

Each member of the family, its founders, donors, volunteers, and scholarship students, is like the stars that my eyes observe tonight, without a doubt beautiful for their matchless spirit which permits them to appear here without selfishness and share the sparkle of their soul... Today I tell them, thank you.

Evelyn, 21, Medical Student

·················

I am studying at the university to be a doctor. In my free time, I do volunteer work with a medical organization. I work with this group because I like to help others in emergency situations. My father was the director of this group before he died four years ago.

For me, the scholarship program is the best gift that God could have given me in my life. It provides hope for a better life for me and my family. It opens a door that enables us to be the people who we want to become. More than that, it provides hope for change for my future patients and hope for a better health care system in the country.

The scholarship program conducts workshops that I like very much. These workshops support all of us and teach us ethics, morality, self-esteem, and other values. We all appreciate the immense help with which the scholarships bless us. Otherwise we would not be able to fulfill our dreams. My hope for the future is to become a good and ethical doctor, to lessen my patients' suffering, and to cure their illnesses. I hope in the future to help the program by sponsoring scholarships myself so that other young people can fulfill their dreams the way I hope to fulfill mine.

●●●●●●●●●●●●●●●●●

Interest in the scholarship program has increased with time as young people observe the effectiveness of the in-country staff workshops, a sustained financial commitment to the scholarship program, and the successes of those who have graduated. Nevertheless, student awareness of their lack of resources, their dedication to achieving success, and their gratitude to others for the help they receive have remained constant over the years.

# CHAPTER 11
## LISIA: FROM DROPOUT TO WIFE AND MOTHER

> "Leaving school may not be the end, it may be the beginning." - Basil O'Leary, a college professor, classroom communication, 1966

Not all of the scholarship students have been successful—at least in terms of the usual metric (i.e., graduation from high school or college followed by a good job). A few students have not maintained acceptable grades to continue in the program. In addition, a few families of students were forced out of neighborhoods and high schools by street gang activity and could not continue in the scholarship program.

Nevertheless, even those who do not graduate benefit from the education they received while attending school. An increased appreciation for education can reverberate throughout the family and across generations to come. Moreover, every year in school for a young adolescent, especially for young women, may be another year to mature before starting a family.

We sponsored Lisia for 4 years of high school from which she successfully graduated. After 3 years of medical school, she clearly was not going to be able to succeed. Although she worked hard, her grades were not sufficiently acceptable to stay in the rigorous medical program. A high percentage of students attending medical school in El Salvador do not graduate.

Lisia is from a good family that John and I got to know well over the 7 years we sponsored her in school. We also got to know other families that lived in the general community. One memorable man was Guillermo, a subsistence farmer and father of 10 children, including one particularly cute set of young, identical twin girls. Guillermo walked with a severe limp. He had fallen off a freight train in Mexico many years previously in a failed attempt to enter the United States. Part of his foot was severed on the rail tracks, and he returned to his home in El Salvador.

Lisia's father, Paulo, is an honest and likeable subsistence farmer. He and his wife, Melva, were resourceful in raising their three children, Carlos, Lisia, and Elsie. For extra income, Paulo and Melva operated a small store in their front yard that was popular in the community for soda drinks, snacks, and sundries. They were industrious and interested in getting the best education they could for their children.

Carlos graduated from high school and had a girlfriend. He is bright and talented. He left El Salvador in the mid-2000s to live and work with an uncle in the United States. He was an undocumented waiter at a restaurant for about 5 years.

Although his job was for low wages, Carlos saved what money he could and sent it home to his parents. Such funds are referred to as "remittances," in which migrants working and living in one country send funds to relatives living in their home country. Remittances are a large source of income to millions of people worldwide who live in developing countries. Consequently, remittances influence immigration policies within Central American and other developing countries as political interests seek to preserve revenue streams (Wolfe, 2017).

A large percentage (about 15% to 20%) of El Salvador's GDP is based on remittances received from Salvadorans living in other countries, especially the United States. With the remittances from Carlos, Paulo and Melva built a beautiful, four-room house on their property.

Carlos, however, reported being very lonely in the United States. He constantly feared he would be discovered as an undocumented worker and deported. He often isolated himself at home when he was not working.

Carlos returned to El Salvador and married his high school girlfriend many years ago. With the money he earned in the United States and the business skills he had acquired, he opened a restaurant in a large city in El Salvador. The restaurant was a success, and Carlos opened two more restaurants, which were also successful business ventures. He now has two small children and employs friends and family members in his business.

After Lisia left medical school, she married a man who she met at the university and who was from the general area where her family lived. They moved to Spain where her husband obtained work. They had a son who Lisia was intent on giving the opportunity of a good education. The experiences and attitudes she acquired in school serve her well as a wife and mother.

Two years ago, Melva had saved enough money to visit her daughter and grandson, who she had never met, in Spain. This trip was Melva's first time on an airplane, and she was traveling alone. Upon her arrival, the Spanish authorities determined that her visa was not legitimate for some reason. They would not allow Melva to enter the country. Melva was required to get on another plane and return to El Salvador without seeing her daughter or grandson. This was a stressful experience for Melva and a tremendous loss of money spent on airfare.

On the return flight from Spain, Melva suffered a massive heart attack and died when the plane stopped in Guatemala. The family was devastated by Melva's death.

# CHAPTER 12
## HOPE: THE POOR STRUGGLE TO LIVE

...........................................................

> "The church is worth little in terms of money or politics but has great value because of the hope. . . . The poorest compesino and the humblest woman of the village, simply by living this hope and this faith, by praying to God, by educating their children, and by bearing witness to their hope, are equal collaborators with the powerful in the construction of the Kingdom of God. . . . This kingdom of God has already come. It is in your hearts." - Saint Oscar Romero, in *The Scandal of Redemption*, edited by Carolyn Kurtz, 2018

I have met many dozens of individuals over the years who were not in our scholarship program through Mike Jenkins and others. Hope is one such person. I met Hope when she was 12 years old. She was the daughter of a woman working in a bakery in Mike's town outside of the capital many years ago. Mike's group sponsored the bakery and trained several women in skills related to baking and running a small business to increase their income.

Hope's family lived in a humble, three-room home. She did not know her biological father. Her mother, Rubia, had seven children with six different men. When I first met Hope, she lived with her mother, a much older stepfather, and six younger siblings.

A couple of years later, Hope's stepfather discovered that Rubia was having an affair. In anger, he left her, took five of the children, and moved to another part of El Salvador. The stepfather had been the primary financial provider for the family. Hope remained in the village with her mother and younger brother, Francisco. They were forced to move to an even more impoverished one-room structure with no electricity or running water.

Hope was religious and attended Catholic Mass without fail every Sunday. She loved to read, and for a few years I regularly brought books in Spanish for her. She appreciated the books, and we discussed the stories.

Hope valued education and made several friends in grade school and high school. After graduating from high school, she held temporary jobs, such as a nanny to a family, to support herself and bring an income to her family.

Hope met and fell in love with Mario, a young man working as a carpenter in the village. They moved in together with his family and had their first son within two years. Rubia left the village to live with her mother in another part of El Salvador.

Although the process of gang occupation in regions may vary, the transformation of this village from a gang-free zone to a gang-infested area was an insidious process that occurred over a couple of years. For over 11 years, we visited this peaceful village before the gangs moved into the area. The village occupied a large area with over 10,000 residents. We typically visited El Salvador twice a year and would stay a week or two with Mike and Susie. We traveled freely throughout the region and visited homes without fear of violence or gang activity.

Initially, gang members took up residence in the village in small numbers, but this expanded over time. Extortions started at a small level and gradually increased. They divided the village into two separate, warring gang territories (i.e., MS-13 and the 18th Street gangs) with clearly recognized boundaries. Gang members with cell phones marked and patrolled the territories. The gangs increased in members, power, and lethality over time.

Murders, infrequent at first, increased in numbers. The gangs periodically killed members of other gangs, but also those extorted or those who were innocent and without gang involvement. It became obvious to all that failure to pay renta to the gangs may result in death.

In reaction, the government authorities sometimes engaged in military/police sweeps of areas, arresting suspected gang members or possibly engaging in violent actions against gang members. A few years ago, seven gang members (and one possibly innocent bystander) were killed in a single combined police/military action in Mike's village. A government inquiry exonerated the police in this incident.

Those suspected of cooperating with the authorities were in special danger. Silence is a code that is strictly enforced by the gangs to protect their activities.

Gang territories expanded in the village and the surrounding area. Mike and other residents would tell us which streets could be entered safely and which were under gang control and could not be entered. Residents sometimes had to request permission from gang leaders to enter certain areas or engage in specific business activities. Terrified residents fearing gang retribution for whatever real or imagined reason left the area and sought refuge in another part of the country.

Gang actions meant to intimidate and control inhabitants could include beatings, outright threats, or corpses (sometime mutilated or beheaded) dumped in public places. We once passed a murdered victim surrounded by police authorities along the highway on the way to one of our student meetings.

The gang control of a region often amounts to another governing authority. Gangs may set curfews on communities, which are strictly obeyed and enforced. They regularly collect extortion monies from businesses and business persons in their territories. A middle-class businessman, who was an acquaintance of ours, reported paying weekly extortion money to a young girl sent by the gangs to his workplace. He adamantly maintained that he would be killed if he did not pay. When temporarily hospitalized for a medical condition, gang leaders entered his hospital room demanding to know who would pay renta to them if he was unable to work. He lived in constant fear.

Increasingly, gangs target private guards or police officers for assassination. Two years ago, a police officer was assassinated in front of his 7-year-old son by three armed men. News of the killing petrified residents. Most people were too frightened to even discuss the killing for fear that neighbors or others overhearing their conversation could inform gang members who would mark them as talking too much or possibly talking to authorities.

Moreover, many individuals fear that gang members bribe some police authorities. They fear any information provided to the police may not be held in confidence but rather shared with gang members who would then seek revenge against them. Not surprisingly, many residents learning of the police officer's murder desire to leave their homes and escape the violence that may eventually engulf them.

Hope's brother, Francisco, was not a gang member, but he drifted aimlessly in life and hung around known gang members. He was not a good student and dropped out of grade school. He lived on the streets, supporting himself by begging and engaging in marginal enterprises. Francisco was arrested in a periodic sweep conducted by police authorities and placed in prison.

Hope described visiting the prison to see Francisco. She was upset and frightened by the prison's crowded, violent conditions. The prison, as are many prisons, is controlled by gangs. The authorities try to separate prison populations by gang affiliation to reduce conflict (Wolfe, 2017). This segregation may lead to greater gang control in which new members may be more easily recruited and in which gang leaders may still dictate gang activities both within prison and on the streets outside of prison (Wolfe, 2017; Martinez et al., 2016). Current government efforts are attempting to limit gang communications so imprisoned leaders cannot control gang activities outside of prison.

Francisco told Hope on one prison visit that she must pay $10 per month to the gang leadership in the prison or he would be regularly beaten by gang members. Although difficult, Hope paid the extortion as best she could.

Eventually, Francisco was released from prison and returned to life on the streets in the village. About 1 year later, Francisco was murdered as he walked a village street with a gang member who was also killed in a drive-by shooting by gang rivals. Hope never discovered if Francisco was an intended target of the shooting or if he was an innocent bystander who was in the wrong place at the wrong time. Francisco was 19 years old when he died, and Hope was in severe grief about the loss of her brother.

Hope had a second son at age 22. Soon afterward, Mario left Hope for another woman he met in the village. Mario and his mother wanted to take custody of Hope's two young toddlers. Hope went to live with her mother and attempted to visit her two sons and regain custody. Two of Mario's brothers were gang members in the village. They threatened Hope with death if she were to appear in the village or try to regain custody of her children.

With time, Mario voluntarily gave up custody and the two children returned to live with Hope. However, in a court proceeding in which Hope was trying to get support from Mario to raise the children, one child expressed the wish to live with his father and grandmother in the village. Much to Hope's horror, the judge awarded one child to Mario and the other to Hope.

Hope lived with her mother, grandmother, son, and other relatives in a small house. For a time, she contemplated making an attempt to enter the United States with her son. Hope's closest friend in high school had entered the United States as an undocumented immigrant several years previously. According to Hope, her friend was successfully attending school, working, and building a life for herself. Typically, destitute people in Central America believe that entering the United States would mean a life of physical safety and a path out of grinding poverty.

The friend advised Hope to leave El Salvador and attempt the perilous journey north, but Hope decided such an action would be too dangerous. She built a small addition to the house for herself and her son and started a small business selling homemade food along a highway to support herself and her family.

Hope is currently in her late 20s. I have not seen her for over 3 years. The last I heard was that she has a new boyfriend living with her, and she is trying to support her family. I hope to see her again someday. I wonder if she has books to read and if her son shares her love of reading.

# CHAPTER 13
# "KILL ME HERE": TERROR ON A BUS

....................................................

"Unfortunately, I live in a society of few opportunities...full of violence and many aspects that should not exist."
- Jorge, a scholarship student

"Trauma robs the victim of a sense of power and control; the guiding principle of recovery is to restore power and control to the survivor. The first task of recovery is to establish the survivor's safety."
- Judith Herman, *Trauma and Recovery*, 1997/2015

Street gangs control territories dominating a large part of both rural and urban areas of El Salvador. Police authorities have little or no control over these areas. People, however, must travel to markets, work, and school through these dangerous territories. The primary mode of transportation in Central America is by bus. The typical fare is about $1 for a trip. As incomes are generally meager, transportation costs are high for the average person.

Cash is king in El Salvador. Few people use credit cards. Digital payment cards for transportation do not exist. Checks also are used rarely. Thus, the average person is usually carrying some cash to navigate the transportation systems and daily market activities.

Street gangs extort most bus companies, which is a major source of income for them (Wolfe, 2017; Martinez et al., 2016). In addition, the bus drivers and passengers are frequently robbed. Most people have stories of being robbed on buses, sometimes more than once. It is an ongoing hazard, especially for bus drivers. Typically, three or more thieves rob buses, with one person in the front, another in the back near another exit, and a third collecting peoples' valuables.

Individuals are careful not to travel with unnecessary valuables (jewelry, watches, or excess cash) and often travel in groups. Nevertheless, there is usually some danger. Tourists or US government personnel are regularly advised to avoid public transportation. When Peace Corps volunteers were in the country, they were advised to limit any travel by bus and not to travel to San Salvador. Mike Jenkins and others have told us stories of robberies or shootings on buses in which innocent people were shot in the crossfire between rival gang members or someone was mistaken for a rival gang member.

Our students face significant perils while traveling for their education. Many students live in areas controlled by gangs and are under constant threat of theft, extortion, sexual assault, or coercion to join gangs.

Students must rise early to get to and from the university. Most students begin their day at 4 or 5 a.m. Classes at one major university start at 6:30 a.m. and typically continue until the afternoon. There are few school buses in El Salvador, so students usually rely on public transportation. Students often live in rural areas, and bus rides to and from the universities, which are typically located in urban areas, may be as long as 2 hours. Once home, students may have chores to do for the family in addition to any academic assignments. They may not get to sleep until late in the evening.

In addition to bus rides, travel sometimes involves long walks, which can put students in jeopardy if they must cross gang territories. Whatever the mode of traveling for their education, some students report being robbed occasionally of their cell phones and any money they carried. Some students have been robbed several times in a year. If they can afford it, students may rent rooms or live with relatives or friends close to the university to avoid the risks of travel.

Women are in special jeopardy when traveling in El Salvador because of the possibility of violent sexual assault. One 27-year-old woman in the scholarship program, Flores, was traveling home alone from the university where she was studying business administration. An obvious gang member armed with a knife boarded the bus that Flores was riding.

The man demanded that Flores get off with him at the next stop where other gang members were waiting for him. Flores immediately recognized this ultimatum as a terrifying and dangerous demand. She knew from previously reported incidents on buses that going with gang members may result in her rape and murder with her body unlikely to be found. Flores realized that acceding to his demand was not possible. She refused to go with the knife-wielding man, indicating to him and the other passengers on the bus that if he was going to kill her to "kill me here."

Flores was adamant. She was ready to die rather than leave the bus. The man persisted in threatening her, but Flores stayed firm in her resistance and prepared to physically resist him. Other passengers on the bus also knew what it likely meant if she left with the man. Some passengers began to protest, and more passengers gradually voiced their concern.

It was a tense and terrifying few moments. To physically force Flores to leave the bus with him would take time and would not have been easy. She was ready to fight for her life. Many murders in Central America happen in private locations without any witnesses. In fact, witnessing a murder is a terrifying prospect for many people. Gangs prioritize killing witnesses of murder to prevent any possibility of being identified and targeted by the police or others for retribution or extrajudicial killing. Mike told us of an incident in his village in which a woman who reported to the police a murder that she witnessed was found murdered in her home the next day.

Flores sensed that her best chance of survival was to remain in the presence of many witnesses. To kill Flores on the bus would have been risky for the armed attacker. The bus was filled with people, and their collective protest was real. Anxious moments passed. The man eventually relented and left the bus without Flores. Flores was not physically harmed and survived the ordeal because of her quick, courageous resistance.

This incident demonstrates the constant physical insecurity in which individuals, especially women, may find themselves in El Salvador (Wolfe, 2017; Lobo-Guerrero, 2017). The incident also shows the resilience and fortitude of our students in fighting for their education. Unlike most people in other developing or developed countries, our students may find themselves in physical peril while striving for an education.

Although Flores was not actually attacked physically, this incident traumatized her. She had to cope with the psychological harm done to her in the days, weeks, months, and years to come. Flores shook with anxious emotions while retelling the story some time later to Tony Gasbarro. Typical of reactions following trauma (Herman, 1997/2015), Flores suffered from a variety of symptoms as well as a loss of trust in her physical safety and relationships. Flores' anxiety level rose sharply on subsequent bus trips, which she had to take to continue her education. Gone was the sense of safety she experienced prior to the terrifying event on the bus.

Flores needed time to recover a greater sense of personal security when traveling. Much time usually has to pass before severely traumatized individuals regain a less anxious, more manageable sense of safety following a physically threatening event. Furthermore, this traumatic incident raised a terrifying warning for our other students and for all other travelers in El Salvador, especially women. The next chapter discusses other traumatic events and reactions to them in El Salvador.

# CHAPTER 14
# MENTAL ILLNESS AND TRAUMA

"To study psychological trauma is to come face to face with human vulnerability in the natural world and with the capacity for evil in human nature. To study psychological trauma means bearing witness to horrible events. When the events are natural disasters or 'acts of god,' those who bear witness sympathize readily with the victim. But when the traumatic events are of human design, those who bear witness are caught in the conflict between victim and perpetrator. It is morally impossible to remain neutral in this conflict. The bystander is forced to take sides."

- Judith Herman, *Trauma and Recovery*, 1997/2015


"What goes right in childhood predicts the future far better than what goes wrong."

- George E. Vaillant, *Aging Well*, 2002


On a warm June day many years ago, the COAR orphanage called Mike Jenkins while I was staying with him for 2 weeks and asked him for a favor. A grossly psychotic, homeless man was hanging around the orphanage trying to see his four sisters who were residents there. They requested that Mike get the man's mother (who lived near Mike) and bring her to the orphanage to remove him.

Mike and the orphanage know the family. Mike tells me the mother, Yesinia, also periodically experiences psychotic symptoms, such as delusions and hallucinations, which are characteristic of severe mental illness, such as schizophrenia. When she takes medication provided by a local clinic, Yesinia does not experience severe psychotic symptoms. When she is not on medication, Yesinia may be psychotic and highly inappropriate. On one occasion, Yesinia threatened her neighbors with a machete; her neighbors are now wary of her. Yesinia has seven children, four of whom were in the orphanage because, given her disability, she was unable to care for them.

Some researchers suggest that persons with schizophrenia may have better outcomes in developing countries than more developed countries for several reasons (Westermeyer, 1993). One reason includes the fact that they generally remain with and are supported by extended families who often provide good care and love for them (Westermeyer, 1993). In contrast, formal psychiatric care in developing countries may lack resources for those who need hospitalization. Mike told me that the only psychiatric hospital in the country was in terrible condition. It was understaffed and overpopulated. Patients were ignored and not cared for properly.

Many of the mentally ill who cannot live with extended families must fend for themselves on the street. Psychological treatment may be expensive and difficult to get for the severely mentally ill in both developing and developed countries of the world. The chronic and severely mentally ill frequently are unable to financially support themselves and may drift over time to lower class standing or marginal impoverished neighborhoods (Gottesman, 1991; Westermeyer, 1993).

We picked up Yesinia and drove to the orphanage. We found her 18-year-old son, Willie, on a street outside the orphanage. He was disheveled, confused, and appeared to be chronically mentally ill. The son agreed to get into the car and go home with his mother. We drove them to Yesinia's home where he could get something to eat, clean clothes, a shower, and have a place to stay and rest for a time. This appeared to be a short-term solution because Yesinia was unable to care for him in her home and his illness required more intensive treatment.

## TRAUMA IN EL SALVADOR

..............................

Willie and Yesinia experience severe, psychotic symptoms characteristic of schizophrenia. There are various course outcomes for schizophrenia and other severe psychotic disorders. Some people experience complete or moderate recoveries, others experience an episodic course of illness, and others suffer a profoundly serious and disabling, chronic course of illness (Westermeyer & Harrow, 1988; Westermeyer, 1993). Both environmental factors and genetic-biological factors influence the development of schizophrenia and other severe mental illnesses such as bipolar I disorder (manic depression), severe depression, and schizo-affective disorders (Gottesman 1991; Ritsner & Gottesman 2011).

In addition to care for the severely, chronically mentally ill, a primary mental health issue in El Salvador and many other countries of the world experiencing extreme violence and destruction (such as Afghanistan, Guatemala, Honduras, Iraq, Syria, and Venezuela) is related to trauma. Trauma refers to the emotional response to a terrible event like physical or sexual abuse, accidents, or national disasters (Voisin, 2019). Trauma may also refer to emotional responses generated by indirect violent incidents and threats, and the various observations or witnessing of trauma (Herman, 1997/2015) or to discrimination or social marginalization (Voisin, 2019).

Historically, the importance of trauma has been ignored or forgotten by the mental health profession due to political forces intent on protecting perpetrators or deflecting the fact that abuse of vulnerable populations may be so widespread (Herman, 1997/2015). A major shift in American psychology in the last 30 years or more has been the recognition that trauma is a major mental health issue that is widespread throughout the world and needs to be assessed, prevented, and treated (Brown, 2008; Herman, 1997/2015; Perry, 2008).

For virtually all mental illnesses, genetic or biological factors interact with environmental stressors such as trauma or other life events and influence the development of psychopathology. The multifactorial interactions of biological/genetic strengths and vulnerabilities and environmental assets and liabilities are complex

(Gottesman, 1991). The weightings of different contributing biological and environmental factors vary by disorders and individuals. Depression, anxiety, disassociated states, post-traumatic stress disorders, personality disorders, immature defenses, and other symptoms and disorders may be particularly influenced by trauma and neurological responses to trauma in addition to potential biologic/genetic factors (Perry, 2008).

A large number of Salvadorans have been traumatized by the extensive incidence of violence, extortion, rape, torture, daily threats, and other stressors. Individuals must find a way to cope in an environment where violence is common and can occur at any moment in their daily lives. They must continually navigate a social context where fear of violence is ubiquitous. The biographies of our scholarship students and others presented in this book illustrate the extent that these adolescents and young adults experience violence, witness violence, or must endure the threat of violence. These students must not only cope with issues of poverty and an inferior primary school education, but with the constant threat of extortion and violence in their everyday travels to school or in their communities under the control of powerful, violent street gangs.

Herman (1997/2015) describes the history of trauma in psychology and the usual trauma recovery process. She argues that the recovery process requires successive periods of 1) safety from the trauma; 2) remembrance and mourning of the trauma; and 3) reconnection with significant others following the trauma. Trauma often precipitates a lack of trust in the environment or of other people who perpetrated the trauma or did not protect the individual from trauma. Control over one's environment is a key psychological issue involving recovery. Herman (1997) writes:

> The core experiences of psychological trauma are disempowerment and disconnection from others. Recovery, therefore, is based upon the empowerment of the survivor and the creation of new connections. Recovery can take place only within the context of relationships; it cannot occur in isolation.

A major issue for many individuals in El Salvador who are traumatized is that the first stage of safety may not be completely established. Recovery usually requires a sense that one is physically safe and beyond the threat of being harmed again. A constant, perceived threat exists for many in El Salvador where each day a person may not feel safe traveling or living in the community.

Moreover, a steady stream of information involves violence in the news or incidents of violence involving acquaintances, personal friends, or family members in the individual's immediate environment. Many Salvadorans experience a constant threat of violence or a continuing extorting relationship where tribute must be regularly paid and may be increased at any time. Failure to pay may mean a death sentence.

To better establish a sense of safety, our scholarship program emphasizes individual empowerment and a network of safe, supporting relationships to diminish trauma or the effects of trauma on lives. Each student chooses their area of study and receives financial support to achieve their goals. The continually supportive, regular relationships in successively scheduled meetings with the in-county staff are crucial to discuss any trauma or other types of disruptive events that take place in the students' lives.

The in-country staff educates students about trauma and strategies for coping with trauma and empowers them to discuss traumatic events if they so choose. The staff also makes efforts to discuss and anticipate any conflicts or traumatic events in the future. They may discuss alternative travel plans or living options to create safer environments for the students. They discuss options to cope with family illnesses, loss, or trauma that may impede learning. Students find safe, supporting, protective networks with the staff and other students where they may share experiences and connect with a caring, trusted community.

In discussing the history of trauma in psychology, Herman (1997/2015) maintains that the effective treatment and recognition of trauma requires a social/political movement. In the first chapter of her book, Herman maintains that the history of trauma in psychology has often been repressed or forgotten by political forces intent on protecting perpetrators. Such forgetting poses a constant danger to recognizing, preventing, and treating trauma in the future. She warns:

> Without a political movement, it is never possible to advance the study of psychological trauma. The fate of this field of

knowledge depends upon the fate of the same political movement that has inspired and sustained it over the last century. (Herman, 1997/2015)

In part, Herman refers to the Vietnam War and recent military history, which sparked awareness of the deleterious impact of combat on psychological adjustment and relationships. Rather than viewing post-traumatic combat stress as moral failure, veterans have begun to receive the compassion and treatment they need.

Herman also refers to the women's liberation movement, in which the widespread prevalence of domestic violence and sexual and physical assaults of women and children across many countries, including the United States, has been recognized. Surveys have documented that 25% or more of women report being sexually assaulted in various countries, including the United States (Herman, 1997/2015). The Me Too movement and Black Lives Matter movement are further iterations of political movements to recognize, treat, and prevent trauma.

The widespread trauma experienced by many individuals in El Salvador, as well as Afghanistan, Guatemala, Honduras, Myanmar, Somalia, Syria, Venezuela, Yemen, and other developing or war-torn countries, must be recognized by political/social entities to begin to prevent trauma and mitigate its effects. While the effects of trauma are often obvious for individuals seeking asylum at the US border, often less apparent and recognized are the large numbers of people who suffer similar traumatic events and yet remain in Central

American countries.

The process of recovery from trauma requires time for the various stages described above to occur. The healing process applies not only to individuals but to the collective culture of the country as well. Through the efforts of mental health professionals such as Judith Herman, Laura Brown, Bruce Perry, George Vaillant, and many others, research and treatment for individuals suffering from trauma has increased and is now a greater focus of concern in clinics, hospitals, and training programs.

Nevertheless, we must devote additional resources to understanding and treating trauma at the collective level of countries and societies as well as at the individual level of personal therapy and counseling. We know less about the effects of trauma at the collective, nation level than we do at the individual, therapeutic level.

Current cohorts that have experienced violence in civil war and in gang activities in El Salvador require the passage of time to significantly establish a sense of safety, reconnection, and healing. The people of El Salvador as a whole have been badly traumatized. Coping and healing must occur at both the individual and collective levels. This process requires a benign political/social context.

Herman (1997/2015) suggests the process of individual recovery involves would-be-helpers being a "witness" to the trauma rather than a "rescuer." By these words Herman means that trauma involves the feeling of helplessness or disempowerment at its core on the part of trauma victims. The well-meaning helper may make the traumatized individual feel more powerless by "rescuing," or over-caring in a manner that makes the individual feel even more helpless or ever more dependent on the caregiver or therapist (Herman, 1997/2015). Effective treatment involves empowering individuals so they are less dependent upon the therapist or caregivers.

In recounting the trauma in the safety of a therapy session, the individual does not carry the burden of the trauma alone. According to Herman (1997/2015), a "crime" has occurred and the would-be helper (or other observer) becomes a "witness" to the abuse borne by the individual. Whereas excessive rescuing weakens survivors, the witnessing process instead empowers them. The survivor is not alone.

Similarly, at the public, collective level, these traumatic stories in Central America or elsewhere become a matter of public record that may, to some extent, be a palliative to traumatized individuals or to society at large. In this context, the life stories in this book give "witness" to the trauma experienced by the students and others who have remained in El Salvador. By extension, they represent similarly traumatized individuals in other Central American countries, other war-torn or violent countries, and violent, marginalized communities in the United States. Although often painful to hear, their stories must be told, dear reader, for you to bear witness to traumatic events and thereby facilitate justice being done and further healing to occur.

Most importantly, the quote that starts this chapter by George Vaillant (2002) suggests that, although trauma may play a pernicious role in psychological development, the positive influence of loving people over long periods of time overcomes or diminishes the effects of trauma or inoculates one from extreme reactions. Based on rigorous longitudinal research in follow-ups of the same individuals for more than 60 years, Vaillant demonstrates that the positive loves that individuals have experienced in life are more important for human development across the life span than the negative or traumatic events in their lives (Vaillant, 2002, 2012).

Our scholarship students come from strong, loving extended families. They are physically and mentally healthy and are psychologically prepared to learn. They have demonstrated success in school and in life before entering our program. They continue to manifest that resilience despite facing difficulties or new traumas along the way.

The scholarship program tells them that they are not abandoned to violent, impoverished conditions. Their fellow students, family members, the in-country staff, and, indeed, donors in the United States personally care about them, believe in their abilities, and support them reaching their educational goals as well as in healing from traumatic events in their young lives.

# CHAPTER 15
# ALBERTO: ESCAPE FROM GANG LIFE

∙∙∙∙∙∙∙∙∙∙∙∙∙∙∙∙∙∙∙∙∙∙∙∙∙∙∙∙∙∙∙∙∙∙∙∙∙∙∙∙∙∙∙∙∙∙∙∙∙∙∙∙∙∙∙∙∙∙∙

"I have two choices: the gangs and death or education and life." -Henri, a 20-year-old scholarship student

"Brothers, you are part of our own people. You are killing your own brother and sister compesinos, and against any order a man may give to kill, God's law must prevail: 'You shall not kill." . . . It is time now for you to reclaim your conscience and obey your conscience rather than the command to sin. . . . In the name of God, then, and in the name of this suffering people whose laments rise up each day more tumultuously toward heaven, I beg you, I beseech you, I order you in the name of God: stop the repression!"

- Saint Oscar Romero, in a homily speaking directly to the army on the day before he was assassinated, March 23, 1980, in *The Scandal of Redemption*, edited by Carolyn Kurtz, 2018

Cindy successfully graduated from college in our scholarship program over 10 years ago. We visited her family many times over the years. Her father, Maximillian, is a remarkable man who labored as a subsistence farmer on a plot of land outside a small village. He is a wise village elder who the community regularly sought for counsel.

Don Max worked as a medical assistant for a local Catholic social service organization. He regularly traveled a wide area around his home as a local, medical, home care worker. He dispensed routine medical care and medications and provided medical screenings if needed to refer individuals for more intensive medical care at a local clinic or hospital.

Despite having a fourth-grade education, Don Max was knowledgeable about medical conditions and treatment in the campo. He maintained detailed medical records on hundreds of his patients in a small home office. He attended training workshops at the agency and studied independently to develop his medical knowledge and skills. He assisted at many deliveries and provided first aid care that saved many lives over 25 years of serving his community. I am amazed how one with so little education can make such a huge difference to the medical well-being of a disadvantaged community.

The people of his community love Don Max. He smiles easily and has a gentle and relaxed demeanor. He is reflective and speaks in a way that is respectful of others and respected by others. In addition to Cindy, Don Max has two other children, Santo, his eldest son, and Alberto, his youngest son.

Over the years it became impossible to visit Don Max. Gang members moved into the area, and we were advised not to visit as we had done for so many years. Gradually, extortions increased, and the gang assumed a dominant position in the community.

One of the primary groups that gangs victimize is the gang members themselves. Gang members are primarily impoverished youth from marginalized communities who have not had opportunities for education or employment (Wolfe, 2017; Martinez et al., 2016). Wolfe (2017), in her scholarly work on controlling gang activity in El Salvador, emphasized that prevention, rehabilitation, and job opportunities are keys to controlling gangs and reducing violence.

Most new gang recruits are boys who find a group identity, perceived "jobs," respect from others, and illusory protection in the gang. Furthermore, many are forced to join gangs under threat of physical harm. Those who join gangs are at great risk for an early death or imprisonment. Failure to respect or follow gang leaders' commands may result in the member's execution. The process is destructive for gang members themselves and those victimized by them (Wolfe, 2017; Martinez et al., 2016).

Malkin (2015) describes the life of one former gang member who at age 24 has entered a rehab job program as follows:

> He joined . . . the gang . . . when he was 14 years old, seeking the companionship and sense of community he couldn't find at home. Neither lasted. "Once you have been in it for two, three, four years, it has filled the emptiness you have . . . but then you realize that you're in something serious." The future in a gang is always the same, he said. "At the end is jail, the cemetery or the hospital."

As the gangs entered Don Max's community, acquaintances, friends, neighbors, and extended family members became involved with the gangs. Alberto, who had classmates, friends, and cousins in the gang, was recruited into the gang as well. The process of involvement in the gang culture was insidious for community residents in general.

We had known Alberto as a young boy, years before the street gangs entered his community. He was a fun-loving, affable boy who was somewhat overweight. Alberto was not mean-spirited or aggressive with others. He was close to and loved his family. Nevertheless, as several of his significant peers and cousins joined a local gang, Alberto was forced to join the gang. Given the violent gang culture, it was physically perilous for him not to join the gang.

Families generally do not want their children taking up the gang culture. They know the risks involved. Don Max was gravely concerned about Alberto's recruitment into the gang. Gang members generally respected Don Max, because he was a village elder for so many years and was respected by their families. Don Max had shown kindness and given medical advice to most families in the valley. Gang members knew him as an ally and community elder throughout their childhood. However, the gang culture is a way of life with strict rules of discipline. Alberto was expected to abide by the gang code of conduct.

Alberto often served as a sentry or watchman for the gang. Police authorities, strangers, or rival gang members must be monitored if they encroach upon the gang's territory. Alberto spent nights watching for police activity or strangers to enter his gang's territory. If he spotted anyone potentially compromising gang territory, he would report it up the chain of command. Much of the time spent by adolescents and young men in gangs involve such repetitive activities. Gang life is a waste of human energy and talent.

Over time, some gang members related to or friends with Alberto and his family were killed in battles with the police/army forces or in ubiquitous territorial warfare with other gangs. Alberto's cousins or childhood friends killed others or were killed themselves. Don Max knew it was a matter of time before his son would also become a victim of the endemic violence.

Finally, Don Max had enough. He scraped together financial resources and sought the help of a coyote to migrate his son illegally to the United States. Quitting the gangs is not easy and involves great risk for most gang members in El Salvador. The gang ethos imposes a strict, unforgiving discipline. Through Mike Jenkins, I learned of one individual who left a gang by embracing an evangelical type of born-again Christianity. Others worked their way out by anonymously moving to another part of the country or leaving the country where the gangs could not find them. Other not-so-lucky gang members are murdered in escape attempts or in failing to be sufficiently loyal or obedient to gang leaders.

Keeping strict confidentiality within the immediate family, Don Max arranged for Alberto's escape. He paid a large sum of money to a coyote to see Alberto safely out of El Salvador. Although expensive, the trip involved no guarantees. At any stage of the journey north, Alberto could be caught by authorities and returned to El Salvador without a refund.

Alberto hugged his mother, father, brother, and sister and left the only home he had known for a perilous journey to a new life in a country whose language and culture he did not know. Alberto knew his life was in danger if his fellow gang members found out that he had made this choice.

Later that year, in a sweep of the gang territory, a combined police/military force arrested many young men living in the community. Santo was caught up in the police sweep and was accused of being a gang member who had extorted people in the community. Don Max maintained that his son was too old to be recruited into the gang and so was not a gang member. Don Max claimed that his son's arrest was a miscarriage of justice.

Wolfe (2017) reasons that political forces have played on public fears of gangs in El Salvador. These fears have led to some extreme, right-wing policies that deny protections under law and may lead to extrajudicial arrests or killings. I do not know the merits of Santo's case, which all come as secondhand information to me. Nevertheless, Wolfe (2017) documents the problematic policies in the region. As in the United States, political factions in El Salvador may exploit fear and hatred of gangs for political gain that may lead to suspension of lawful rights and extrajudicial arrests and killings, as well as additional votes in elections. Moreover, the news media may sensationalize gang activities to justify political actions and influence elections by interests controlling the media (Wolfe, 2017).

In any case, Santo can be held in prison for a lengthy time by police authorities without charges being made or a judicial process proceeding. Indeed, Santo was held for over a year in prison and released without a trial. The charges made against him were dropped.

As Wolfe (2017) points out, "mano dura," or hard-handed, draconian policies against gangs in the past have not been effective. A judicial process of widespread arrests without adequate due process may be a deleterious policy for many because the rule of law is sabotaged and extrajudicial processes and executions may increase gang strength and activity (Wolfe, 2017). Moreover, as prisons are often dominated by a gang culture in which gang leaders may control gang behavior both inside and outside the prison, crass arrests of innocent people may make for a fertile recruitment venue for new gang members in prisons (Wolfe, 2017; Martinez et al., 2016).

El Salvador has one of the highest incarceration rates in the world, numbering close to 39,000 inmates. NGOs and other organizations are attempting to rehabilitate gang members in prison, most of whom will eventually be released back into the community. Better control of gangs in El Salvador would involve significant rehabilitation of gang members both in and out of prison.

Several years later, I indirectly learned that Alberto made it to the United States and escaped gang life in El Salvador. He probably lives someplace where he, along with millions of other undocumented immigrants, works in whatever low-paying jobs he can obtain to survive. I do not know if he has applied for asylum, to which he may be entitled. Alberto probably lives in constant fear of deportation to a country where his life would be in jeopardy if he were to return.

Meanwhile, Cindy and Santo help Don Max and their mother earn a living on a farm where they raise several cows. Respecting Don Max, gang members have not retaliated against the family for Alberto's escape from gang membership.

Alberto's story increases my empathy for the tens of thousands of gang members in El Salvador who are caught up in a pernicious, oppressive process that ultimately will destroy many if not most of them. As Henri, one scholarship student told me, "I have two choices: the gangs and death or education and life."

The quote by Saint Romero which begins this chapter was a plea made to the military in a time of numerous murders by the right-wing death squads about 40 years ago. This plea to the common soldier not to kill led to his assassination the next day (Moodie, 2010).

Saint Romero's life history is a profound story central to El Salvador. Selected as a conservative archbishop of San Salvador in 1977, Romero changed after observing social injustices through his priests and others serving under his authority who were involved in social justice activities. The turning point for Romero occurred with the death of a close friend, Father Rutilio Grande, who was shot by gunmen in March 1977 (Romero, 2018; Moodie, 2018).

Father Rutilio Grande was critical of the government and was heavily involved in social justice causes. People suspected that right-wing, government death squads were responsible for his murder. On observing the body of his friend, Romero said: "When I looked at

Rutilio lying there dead I thought, 'If they had killed him for doing what he did, then I too have to walk the same path'" (Romero, 2018). That moment was a radical turning point for Romero (Romero, 2018; Moodie, 2010).

Romero started calling for an investigation into Grande's murder and insisted on addressing other social justice issues that he observed. He directly spoke to the people through weekly homilies that were broadcast by radio from the cathedral as he celebrated Mass each Sunday. A priest who witnessed Romero's activities at the time told me how a large percentage of the people would tune into Romero's homilies each week. Peasants would bring transistor radios to their local church and while attending Mass listen to Romero's broadcasts from the cathedral. His radio audiences grew to include half of San Salvador residents and three-quarters of the rural peasants, despite efforts by the government authorities to shut down the radio broadcasts (Romero, 2018).

Romero promoted social justice initiatives among the poor and confronted government authorities on repressive measures and their refusal to investigate the murders of his priests and others engaged in social justice activities. Given his previous social conservative orientation, Romero's social justice activities during the 3 years of his tenure as archbishop from 1977 to 1980, following the death of his friend, were striking.

Increasingly, governing authorities and right-wing conservative interests saw him as a threat to their regime. The quote by Romero that begins this chapter was spoken the day before he was murdered.

He called on soldiers to stop the violence and not to obey orders to kill others. The next day, on March 24, 1980, a car stopped outside the Hospital Divina Providencia Chapel where Romero was celebrating Mass. The assassin emerged from the car with a gun and from the entrance to the chapel fired into the chest of Romero standing on the altar of the chapel. The killer returned to the car, which sped away. Saint Romero died soon afterward.

Twelve years later the Truth Commission identified right-wing military elements associated with the governing authority as responsible for the assassination. His murderers, however, were never brought to justice.

In death, Saint Romero joined other social change agents, such as Abraham Lincoln, Martin Luther King Jr., and Mohandas K. Gandhi, who spoke truth to powers regarding social injustices and were assassinated to silence them. They are martyrs to noble causes, and their voices have been amplified in history.

Notably, the words by Romero that begin this chapter, although spoken about 40 years ago to military soldiers, retain their meaning if spoken to gang members in El Salvador today. The culture of violence, then as now, continues to take lives. Romero would beg that it stop.

Psychologists defining and studying moral development claim that those who achieve the highest levels of morality are rare. One reason for this rarity is that the highest levels of morality are based on self-chosen principles that transcend the self-interests of the person. The individuals at the highest levels of morality often pay a price for their moral stance because their self-interest is secondary to their moral reasoning. The great nonviolent, social change agents of the 20th century—Martin Luther King Jr., Nelson Mandela, and Mohandas K. Gandhi—put principles of social justice activism above their parochial interests, their personal freedom, and their very lives.

Like King and Gandhi before him, Romero knew his public defiance of oppressive authority may well result in his death. In the weeks before his murder, Romero saw that his death was likely, and in Christ-like fashion he forgave his assassins before they murdered him by telling a reporter:

> You can tell them, if they succeed in killing me, then I pardon them, and I bless those who may carry out the killing. But I wish that they could realize that they are wasting their time. A bishop will die, but the Church of God—the people—will never perish. (Romero, 2018)

Romero, as does Lincoln, King, Mandela, and Gandhi, lives on in the hearts and minds of teeming millions for their principles, ideals, and compassion for others that transcend moments in history. Like them, Romero was a man of action who responded when he saw injustice.

Saint Romero's story is one of heroic change. He changed from being a social conservative to a social justice activist when he saw something that he knew was wrong. He was ready to die for his beliefs. How common is such a transformation? Who has such courage? He then forgave his killers in advance. Such forgiveness and compassion! How is that possible? Where does that come from?

Saint Romero's life story is a beacon for today in demonstrating the possibilities of change and forgiveness. If thousands of gang members are to be rehabilitated, we must hope for their heroic change and remorse for past transgressions. Then we may ultimately emulate Romero and find it in ourselves to forgive them.

Even more, gang members may reject their past actions, feel remorse for harm done to others, and ultimately forgive themselves to achieve a complete rehabilitation. Data on development illustrates the process of law-breaking and violence (or acting out) in youth often being transformed to more mature coping as adults develop a conscience or morality with aging that often condemns earlier transgressions (Vaillant, 1992, 1993, 2012). Not surprising, religious conversions condemning past antisocial impulses (or reaction formation) is often part of this transformation (Vaillant, 1993).

I thought the role of our scholarship students in this change process was well described by one of our students, Diane, as follows:

> "I think our society could change if we change and if we help others change their bad thoughts into good ones."

# CHAPTER 16
# EMPOWERING WOMEN

........................................................................

> "The gender similarities hypothesis holds that males and females are similar on most, but not all, psychological variables. That is, men and women, as well as boys and girls, are more alike than they are different." - Janet Shipley Hyde, "The Gender Similarities Hypothesis," 2005

> "The brothers were brought up to be men. The girls had been reared to get married. . . . 'Any man will be happy with them because they've been raised to suffer.'" - Gabriel García Marquez, *Chronicle of a Death Foretold*, 1982

> "My business makes me feel competent. I feel greater independence and self-respect—as a woman." - A 60-year-old women in a microlending program

A few summers ago, John and I arrived in a small farming community a few miles from Suchitoto, an art and tourist town in central El Salvador. There, we visited a microlending organization of women. The NGO that we work with on the scholarship program also administers other community-building projects, including a microlending program organized into several separate groups of women in different locations. We have made similar visits over the years to enhance our understanding of community activities that increase wealth and employment in the country.

Although the microlending program is separate from the scholarship program, the empowerment of women who assume the major responsibility of raising children relates directly to the education of children. Women are often single-parent heads of households in El Salvador and other developing countries and thus play a major role in promoting and valuing education in their families.

Economist Muhammad Yunus (2003) started microlending in Bangladesh to aid poor women. Microlending empowers women to start their own business through small loans. Although some controversy exists over the effectiveness of microlending programs at macro, national levels, these programs targeted for disadvantaged women benefit many families across the globe.

We met 17 women in the microlending group that day, including their president, Lucile, and their treasurer, Magdalene. The women varied in age from their early 20s to late 60s. Their faces and demeanor reflected the effects of weather, poverty, and hard work over many years, but also showed character, integrity, and dignity.

Small loans of $50 to $200 had been given to each member of this microlending group. Each invested the money in their small business. Elected officers of the group carefully monitored the allocation of funds. As businesses thrived, loans with interest were repaid and the capital of the microlending group accumulated to make new loans for other members. The women and officers keep a careful accounting of the funds for lending. Together, they approve future projects for allocating funds.

The microlending project works like a bank without the building. Consequently, expenses and interest rates for the loans are low. The small interest paid goes back to benefit the group as new money for loans for individual businesses, community projects, and celebrations for the group.

Each woman shared her story as we went around the group to hear each testimony. One woman borrowed $50 to buy clothing materials from which she makes handbags that she sells in the open market in Suchitoto. With her profits, she buys more material to make more handbags as the number of handbags and profits increase.

Another woman borrowed $150 to buy chickens. She runs an egg selling business that adds to the nutrition intake of the community and increases her profits. Another woman described a small food shop she runs out of her home. She sells soda and sandwiches made from the raw materials she was able to buy with the loans. The stories went on as each woman recounted the small businesses started and how each business has grown to provide a larger part of the family income. It is a program of capitalism at its best.

One woman described her business of making aprons, towels, and napkins that she sells to stores in the area. She said: "My business makes me feel competent. I feel greater independence and self-respect—as a woman."

Typical of microlending programs, the money borrowed is

repaid in full. These women know each other well. They are neighbors and friends who depend on each other for emotional and material support. To default on these loans is unthinkable in terms of their close working relationships to each other. In listening to their stories, I marvel at how far so little money can go to help a family feed, clothe, and shelter itself. Their stories renew my belief in the strength and resilience of these women each time I visit a microlending group.

Some women brought their children with them to the meeting. One woman breastfed her infant, others held their toddlers, and others kept a watchful eye on young children playing nearby. Some of the women are married while others are single heads of households. They provide a strong role model for their daughters—that women can control their own financial lives—and to their sons—that women can be strong and financially independent and deserve the respect of men. Adult male members of the households appreciate the added income to the family, and respect for women increases. Most importantly, as the above statement by one of the women illustrated, the self-respect of the women themselves increases.

Melinda Gates (2019) suggests in her book, *The Moment of Lift*, that the escape from the cycle of poverty in a community is most dependent on the empowerment of women. She describes how women who control the timing and number of their children raise the financial well-being of the family unit. If there are too many children born in succession, the health of the child suffers and creates new and often insurmountable problems for the family.

Moreover, a large number of children may stretch family resources to the breaking point or greatly reduce the ability of a family to provide for itself. The proper number and spacing of children, Gates (2019) argues, makes for a more economically viable development for both children and parents as well as ultimately for the community and country. Women the world over are choosing to have smaller families, as the child mortality rate significantly decreased over the decades (Sachs, 2015).

The women in the microlending group we visited were growing businesses. I now better understand how the economic empowerment of women may best drive forward the economic developmental of a community. The better the resources of the family led by the center of the family—women—the more likely the child will thrive and have an opportunity to physically develop. With physical development, children are better prepared to acquire and take advantage of educational and economic opportunities. They arrive at school physically and emotionally healthy and prepared to learn. Gates (2019) explains that birth control planning and the empowerment of women in choosing how many and when to have children is essential to the economic and educational development of communities and countries.

Anthropologist and psychologist Robert LeVine and his associates at Harvard University provide additional rigorous evidence on the importance of educating women. Their research explored the effects of women's schooling and literacy in four countries: Mexico, Nepal, Venezuela, and Zambia (LeVine et al., 2012). Through direct assessments, they found that maternal literacy and schooling influence declining child mortality and fertility and the communication competence of children. They conclude: "Our findings support the policy message of UNICEF and other agencies claiming that women's schooling is not only beneficial but also essential for health and human development" (LeVine et al., 2012).

Although we have men in our scholarship program, the majority of scholarship recipients are women. Following Gates' wise counsel, as well as evidence from LeVine et al. (2012) and advice from policy makers and our colleague Tony Gasbarro, John and I believe that emphasizing the education of young women is an effective strategy for lifting up a whole community. As always, the stories of the microlending women that we visited inspired us. As we departed, we thanked them for their time and left a donation to add to their lending funds.

Later we had lunch with Lucille and Magdalena at a restaurant in Suchitoto. We learned more about their backgrounds and more about the community we visited. The community is comprised of about 150 families. Gangs are not present in this community, and the women fervently hope that it will remain so. Their children attend a nearby primary school and a high school closer to Suchitoto. A few students attend the university. They have a medical building in the village, but it is not staffed by a doctor or other medical personnel due to the expense involved.

We also learn that many of the older microlending women were combat veterans of the 12-year civil war in El Salvador, fighting on the side of the rebel forces. Magdalena told us that she fought for 12 years with the rebel guerillas against government forces in the mountains during the Salvadoran Civil War. She shared stories of combat, the loss of comrades-in-arms, and incidents where she narrowly escaped death. Magdalena showed us a care-worn photo of herself in her youth in battle dress as a guerilla fighter. Now she fights a new type of war—fighting poverty with other women by building small businesses, products, and wealth. The war is over. The strength, dignity, and integrity of the women we met in the microlending program are etched in my memory.

# CHAPTER 17
# DIALOGUE WITH THE POOR

..............................................................

> "The philosopher . . . ceaselessly searches for moments of incandescence in dialogue where insight occurs. But never does he achieve a final definition of the Good, or justice or friendship." - Basil O'Leary, 1980

> "I am getting more out of this than I am giving." -John Kukankos, Peace Corps volunteer in El Salvador, 1972

Altruistic issues involve the transformation of the donor as well as those who benefit. As time goes by, would-be-helpers and those helped continue to change and develop. Does altruistic giving also benefit the giver in some way?

The 12th-century Jewish philosopher Maimonides discussed the role of the philanthropist in his hierarchy of charitable giving (see Chapter 1). Maimonides (2006) maintained a higher form of helping meant the benefactor was not known to those she helped or did not know who she helped. For Maimonides, giving for a return of fame or fortune defines a less authentic charity or helping relationship. A quid pro quo activity was a lesser form of giving because it was based on self-interest rather than wishing good to others for themselves.

Thus, anonymity characterized his higher levels of charity. Maimonides (2006) described different gradations of anonymity in his eight principles of charitable giving.

One of my closest friends was adamant in maintaining his anonymity in giving to others. He would never disclose his charitable activity to me. I found out about his giving years later through indirect sources. How rare this must be, especially in a society in which tax write-offs for charitable donations are so important.

Nevertheless, after being involved in Project Salvador Scholarship Program for some time, I think Maimonides largely got it wrong. There are other more subtle psychological benefits in any helping relationship apart from obvious returns in fame and fortune.

Helping relationships are rarely one way in nature. Although power differentials always exist and gains from giving may involve selfish motivations or material aggrandizement, those who help others may benefit in many less obvious or unconscious ways. In dialogue, both those more powerful and those less powerful may change and learn from each other, especially in types of giving that does not involve material matter.

A basic assumption of dialogue is that one may learn from the other. We seek the truth but never gain the final, complete truth. It's a process, not an end state. Basil O'Leary (1980) elaborates on the quote that begins this chapter:

> Since there is no absolute Truth in the world, no one can claim its possession. We live in a finite world of relative

"truths"; perceptions of the good life, religions, interpersonal relations, political decisions, science and art, work and leisure, "fair wages." Within such a limited horizon, no one can injure or coerce another to accept his claim to truth.

Dialogue, in its various forms, is the process of working toward the truth. Others can provide insights that have eluded us. We can learn from a variety of others despite power differentials or conflicts.

Political dialogue posits that some truth exists across the political spectrum. Thomas Jefferson understood the split in policy positions along party lines as a never-ending drama to be continually replayed with new issues in subsequent generations. Within certain parameters, policy options, reflecting paradoxes in human nature, ever remain to be arbitrated in the political process. There are always "pros" and "cons" of any policy position, and dialogue is required for compromise or finding common ground for action.

Vaillant (2012), a wise investigator of adult development, maintains generativity, a higher level of development in which the older generation cares for and nurtures subsequent generations, involves older individuals learning from the younger generations while mentoring them. Both parties benefit from a reciprocal relationship and from dialogue with one another.

To truly influence another in dialogue, the mentor must also be influenced or changed in some way by the mentee through their close relationship. Thus, parents learn from their children as well as teach their children. I always love the phrase "the child raises the family," indicating reciprocal parent-child socialization in that the child influences parents while being raised by them. Parents may better develop and transform because of their children. I have seen such miracles in many friends and acquaintances who have become parents. For Vaillant (2002), a key question for parents in assessing generativity is: "What have you learned from your children?"

Similarly, teachers learn from and teach their students. One marker I set for success in teaching each term is how much I learn from my students. The best teaching resource for any teacher is the minds of their students. The more teachers learn in the process of education, the more likely students learn. Paulo Freire (1970/2018) summaries this process as follows:

> Problem-posing education, which breaks with the vertical patterns characteristic of banking education, can fulfill its function as the practice of freedom. . . . Through dialogue, the teacher-of-the-student and the students-of-the-teacher cease to exist . . . and a new term emerges: teacher-student with students-teachers. The teacher is no longer merely the-one-who-teaches, but one who is himself taught in dialogue with students, who in turn while being taught also teach. They become jointly responsible for a process in which all grow.

Therapists also learn much from their clients. There is reciprocity of discovery of self and other in therapy dialogue—in what is known as the "transference" and "counter-transference" of the relationship. For example, Gene Combs (2018) describes learning about the unique context of his clients of color and their struggles with poverty and systematic racism that impact therapy. He became more aware of his own white privileges through his clients' stories. He makes specific recommendations to develop empathy and understanding of minority clients as well as to increase awareness of institutional racisms and actions to combat racism (Combs, 2018).

In addition, Laura Brown (2008) explains that trauma may be experienced in diverse ways by different clients that a therapist needs to better understand for effective treatment. She further maintains that the therapist has much to learn from clients about effective ways individuals cope with trauma. Brown (2018) points out that the therapist needs to learn from clients about the cultural context of the trauma and the unique adaptions made by each client in that context.

Similarly, both Herman (1997/2015) and Vaillant (1992) explain that the therapist learns about the effects vicarious trauma (e.g., listening to distressing material in therapy) has on their own affects, reactions, and mental health. They need social supports, self-care, and good boundaries in doing therapy.

Both Vaillant (1992) and Herman (1997/2015) elucidate that chronic, severe trauma may disrupt relationships, which may include the client's relationship with the therapist. Chronically traumatized individuals, Vaillant explains, are more likely than others to employ immature defenses (such as projection, passive aggression, and acting out), which frequently elicit negative emotions and similar immature defenses in the therapist and others. Thus, the therapist needs to learn, anticipate, and manage negative emotions or potential, immediate, immature defenses in their responses to clients (Vaillant, 1992).

Conversely, therapists also experience positive emotions and relationships that impact their self-learning and development, both personal and professional, in the therapy milieu. Therapists may learn the myriad reciprocal reactions to present and past events of both client and themselves in the therapeutic dialogue. Both grow in the process.

So too do we have much to learn from dialogue with the disadvantaged and oppressed of the world. They have much to teach us. Gates (2019) writes of her continual learning and the transformation of herself and her marriage through her philanthropic work. She attributes a large part of her personal development to her interactions with those she helps through her philanthropic work.

I find the culture and people of El Salvador to be most welcoming. Families warmly invite us into their homes to share meals and to be part of their extended family. With time, John and I became father-like figures to many children, adolescents, and young adults. I do not have biological children, but happily became a padrino to many individuals in El Salvador. With great gratitude, I now have a parental legacy that I didn't think I would be able to have in life.

The Salvadoran students are generous in their support of each other and me. I have learned much from students we have sponsored over the years, their families, the in-country staff, and other people in El Salvador. I have been transformed, supported, and inspired in many ways by knowing them. They have endured despite traumas and disadvantages. They model strengths to me that I doubt I possess.

Through the people of El Salvador, I have become more aware of the opportunities and privileges in my life in the United States that are routinely denied to so many others in the world.

I have learned about more effective interventions. As one student, Nicholas, wrote in a requested essay: "We cannot repay the donation, but we have a way to show you (donors) how to help others."

I better appreciate the diverse cultures of international students who so enrich my classes.

I better understand the immigrants from Central American and other countries who present themselves at the US southern border, and of the traumatic conditions that drive migrations the world over.

I have been able to again connect with Brother Denis Murphy, my high school teacher and friend, and his work at Su Casa Catholic Worker in Chicago. Brother Denis cofounded Su Casa in the early 1990s to provide support and a home for migrants from Central America.

I better sense the struggles of my immigrant grandparents, Michael McDonough and Helen Roach McDonough, and what they must have endured to escape poverty and starvation in late 19th-century Ireland by traveling to America through Ellis Island.

I better understand the psychological impact of trauma on clients who find their way into the clinical therapy practicum sites and internships where my students train to become clinical psychologists.

I better appreciate strengths, mature defenses, and resilience in individuals to overcome barriers to success.

The people of El Salvador have deeply enriched my development beyond words. I now better understand John's quote above from 1972 when he told me: "I am getting more out of this than I am giving."

# CHAPTER 18
# SUMMING UP

........................................................

"The only certain happiness in life is to live for others."
- Leo Tolstoy, *Family Happiness*, 1859/1960

He is forever free who has broken
Out of the ego-cage of I and Mine
To be united with the Lord of Love
That is the supreme state. Attain thou this
And pass from death to immortality
- *Bhagavad Gita*, chapter 2, translated by Mohandas Gandhi, in *Gandhi the man*, by E. Easwaran, 1978

While the traumatic experiences of thousands of desperate individuals escaping Central American countries for asylum in the United States occupies much of the news in recent years, less well known are the life stories of those who remain in these countries and contend with similar circumstances. I hope that this book has given a voice to those adolescents and adults who remain in El Salvador and cope with poverty and a traumatizing violent culture.

Although economic historians debate the timing and reasons (Landes, 1998; Maddison, 2007; Sachs, 2005), unprecedented economic progress over the past few centuries is well documented (Sachs, 2005, 2015; Pinker, 2018). Spurred on by the industrial revolution and breakthrough scientific discoveries that followed, wealth per person alive in constant prices and corrected for inflation increased from about $651 in 1820 to about $5,942 in 2010 (Sachs, 2015). According to Pinker (2018), world wealth (gross world product [GWP]) has grown over 200 times since the beginning of the Enlightenment in the 18th century.

Despite wars, economic recessions and depressions, and pandemics, the improvements have been stunning and unprecedented in human history in GWP and other measures of progress across recent centuries. Child mortality continues to significantly decrease and the length of lives is increasing the world over as medical science continues to control disease and make new discoveries. Thus, the life expectancy of individuals in the United States has grown from about 47 years in 1900 to over 76 years today. The world population has grown from about 500 million in the 16th century to about 1 billion in 1820, to over 7.5 billion today.

In addition, a larger percentage of the world's population continues to work its way out of poverty categories. For the sum total of humankind, wealth continues to accumulate at a historically breathtaking pace over recent decades and centuries (Sachs, 2015; Pinker, 2018).

Nevertheless, wealth is not equally shared. Some easily live in opulence, others live comfortably without fear of starvation, and still others live in extreme poverty, unable to meet basic needs and struggle to survive. Although the percentage of human beings living in poverty has decreased over the years, the number of those still living in extreme poverty range from 1 billion to 2.5 billion depending on one's definition (Sachs, 2015). The great disparity of wealth, both within and among nations, does not relate to moral failings. Rather, economic historians identify a variety of complex, causative factors for wealth inequities (Landes, 1998; Maddison, 2007; Sachs, 2005, 2015), while economists propose new solutions to address inequities and poverty in the world based on scientific inquiry (Banerjee & Duflo, 2019).

One major implication of climate change, the possibility of a nuclear exchange, and the Covid-19 pandemic is that, to a great extent, the countries of the world face mutual problems requiring collective action and cooperation. Pollution and disease do not respect boundaries. The fate of the poor in developing countries is inextricably tied to our well-being. Ultimately, it is in our self-interest to raise the education level and economies in El Salvador and the other developing countries. To address wealth inequities, education, health and climate change issues in the world, 193 nations adopted 17 Sustainable Development Goals (SDGs) in September 2015 (World Bank Group, 2018). The United Nations General Assembly set the SDGs for the year 2030. The SDGs build on the previous United Nations Millennium Goals from 2000 to 2015. They include a list of 169 targets and 232 indicators associated with the goals.

Many of the SDGs are being addressed in one way or another by

NGOs in developing countries such as El Salvador. In particular, the goal of our scholarship program well fits the fourth SDG: to ensure a quality education for all (World Bank Group, 2018).

Education the world over plays a major role in lifting individuals out of poverty and into lives of productivity for themselves and their community. Tony Gasbarro started the Project Salvador Scholarship Program, of which we are one part, in 1998. He has worked tirelessly for over 20 years to sustain and grow the scholarship program.

Since its inception, the Project Salvador Scholarship Program has graduated about 500 students from high school and about 80 students from the university or technical schools with advanced degrees. John and I have sponsored students since 2003 through the scholarship program as well as through efforts with Mike Jenkins and the COAR orphanage. With the help of many donors, we hope to maintain current scholarships and add more students to the scholarship program each year.

The "brain drain" in developing countries, in which well-educated and usually wealthy individuals leave their own countries for better opportunities in other countries, is a major, worldwide issue for underdeveloped countries. A high percentage of college graduates in El Salvador in past years, with the skills and education to build a more economically viable El Salvador, have left the country for better pay and career opportunities in other countries. Indeed, upper- and middle-class, well-educated individuals in El Salvador have career choices. The possibility of leaving El Salvador is increasingly tempting for many individuals wishing to escape the violence with the financial means to do so.

For our scholarship students, and for a large majority of people in the country, leaving El Salvador for better opportunities in a wealthy country is not a viable option. It is difficult to leave El Salvador for another country unless one has sufficient wealth to demonstrate to authorities that they have financial resources or a job waiting for them in the new country. Even after graduation, our students continue to struggle in difficult financial conditions.

Consequently, all of the students who have graduated from college or graduate school through the Project Salvador Scholarship Program have remained in El Salvador to financially help themselves and their families and to build a stronger El Salvador. Although the graduates obtain better paying jobs than they would have otherwise, they are still not wealthy. El Salvador has a high unemployment rate. Our scholarship alumni struggle to find good paying jobs or to start a small business to earn a living.

Change characterizes our lives at different levels. George Vaillant, in his book, *Spiritual Evolution*, describes three different types of co-occurring evolutions: biological, cultural, and individual. Biological evolution proceeds slowly but steadily (Reich, 2018). The brain of a Homo sapiens contains the more primitive, reptilian segments, while the parts of the brain that have come online later in evolution display not only cognitive/language abilities in the neocortex unrivaled among animals, but the so-called positive emotions (e.g., love, empathy, joy, compassion) that continue to expand and evolve (Vaillant, 2008).

Moreover, the brain is the most complex human organ and is subject "to complex interactions not just among genes, proteins . . . but also between individuals and their changing experiences" (Gottesman & Gould, 2003). The plasticity of the human brain is exquisitely sensitive to its environment, especially to relationships with other people.

Cultural evolution concerns information passed on through generations through learning and loving in a shared community rather than a genetic context (LeVine & New, 2008). Cultural evolution is more flexible and rapid than biological/genetic evolution. The progress in cultural evolution may be documented in economic history (Sachs, 2005, 2015), cognitive development and diverse civilizing processes (Pinker, 2018), and maturing political systems (Fukuyama, 1992/2006, 2011). In particular, Pinker (2011, 2018) argues that war, homicides, and other forms of violence have significantly declined over the decades and centuries.

The third type of evolution proposed by Vaillant (2008) is the growth and development of an individual across the human life span, from birth, through childhood, adolescence, young and middle adulthood, and finally old age. Vaillant (2002, 2012), in the longest, prospective follow-ups to date in the field, carefully documents progressive human development in groundbreaking, longitudinal studies, in which he and his colleagues repeatedly assesses the same individuals at different points across more than 60 years of life.

Vaillant (2002, 2008, 2012) reports trends toward greater maturity and positive emotions (or spirituality) with aging. Often, the immature, self-absorbed adolescent becomes, with time, an altruistic, mature, wise adult. In Erikson's (1950/1963) model, an expanding social radius of concern with a wider community frequently concludes with a concern for all humankind rather than a focus on the self or parochial interests.

The self-centered adolescent or striving, competitive young adult becomes the self-less, midlife adult sacrificing for children and the wider community. Vaillant (2002, 2012) demonstrates these changes in rigorous research, as well as the maturing of defenses from such immature defenses as acting out, passive aggression, and projection to the mature defenses of suppression, sublimation, anticipation, humor, and altruism. Older individuals are more likely to display mature defenses, an ease in relationships, generativity, empathy, and other positive emotions in comparison to themselves at earlier periods of their lives. Vaillant (2008) emphasizes that one life period is not necessarily better than another, but rather different aspects of self arise at different points of development.

Vaillant argues that evolution proceeds at the three levels in terms of developing positive emotions (e.g., joy, hope, faith, compassion, forgiveness), which for him are synonymous with spirituality. These three types of evolution are not straight-line, invariant, developmental sequences. There are, of course, diverse individual life courses with negative, primary emotions (e.g., disgust, sadness) intermingled with positive, other-oriented, primary emotions. Some societies regress. Some individuals do not develop or regress. Nevertheless, according to Vaillant (2008), the overall evolutionary positive trends proceed at both the collective and individual levels.

In support of Vaillant's research, I have seen the miraculous development of students we are sponsoring as they mature from adolescents to young adults. Similarly, in my 27 years at Adler University, I have witnessed the development of graduate students in my classes: from their first year to graduation five years later, to productive, professional alumni 15, 20, and 25 years later.

I have observed a similar progressive development in a 57-year, prospective, longitudinal research of men selected for health and assessed in 1959 at age 20 and then reassessed in two follow-ups at the average ages of 53 and 69 (Westermeyer, 1998, 2004, 2013) and most recently in a third follow-up at age 77. If children, adolescents, and young adults are loved, nurtured, and educated in the earliest phases of life, they usually achieve great things, as Vaillant (2002, 2012) maintains, in later phases of life—in later, middle, and older adulthood.

If history is our guide (Pinker, 2011, 2018), El Salvador or other war-torn or extremely violent countries of the world will not continue to experience excessive violence indefinitely.

Furthermore, economic history suggests that poverty will continue to be conquered with less and less of the world's population living in impoverished conditions in the decades and centuries to come (Sachs, 2015; Pinker, 2018). The trend toward the end of poverty continues (Sachs, 2005, 2015). If history is our guide, more educational and career opportunities will continue to emerge for young people and generations yet unborn the world over, including the young students in El Salvador.

In contrast, while poverty and excessive violence are likely time-limited in the long term, the positive benefits of education and good mentoring will endure in the lives of the El Salvador scholarship students and the lives of their children and grandchildren for generations to come. Such a positive investment in human beings cannot be stolen or invalidated like material possessions. It will continue to flourish in ways yet unknown over the next 50 years of their lives and beyond through their children, grandchildren, and their career/community legacy.

The traumatizing incidents occurring in the life histories of most of these students in El Salvador, while having a deleterious impact, may be contained and overcome with assured safety, social connections, positive emotions, and time. As Vaillant (2002, 2012) suggests, the long-term, loving relationships experienced by these students in family and friend relationships, as well as the education that they have earned, are more important for their long-term development than the negative or traumatic events that they have experienced in their young lives. They will not just survive—they will flourish.

Finally, as you already may have guessed, El Salvador stories include my own story. Although not readily observed (as it is always easier to assess others than oneself) has been my own development through my El Salvador experiences. I have changed. I am not the same person that I was when I started visiting the country so many years ago. The people I have met and incidents I have experienced in the country of "The Savior" have changed me for the better. The community of colleagues, friends, students, and their families in living for something larger than the self has been a spiritual awakening for me in which positive emotions flourish. I feel at one with others in a way that transcends personal gain. Although we must be selfish in the right ways in young adulthood to acquire a self to give the next generation in a later, more selfless adulthood (Vaillant, 2002, 2012), many of my earlier strivings to succeed as a young man now seem to me, in retrospect, trivial and often irrelevant.

[margin notes: que lindo es / tener / para dar]

The age-old questions press in on me as always. What is the right way to live? What is important and not important? What is the truth? In the social justice actions, positive emotions and dialogue of a committed community of friends, which includes the students, a pathway is found. No one is more important than someone else involved in the process. We're all in this together. In knowing the students, personal ego disintegrates and compassion and understanding increase. The greater the adversity students overcome daily, the more heroic they appear to me.

The spiritual connection in relation to others transcends to a peaceful feeling of being at one with all and promoting all. Consequently, all spheres of life coalesce in the whole. Everything (e.g., research, teaching, social justice actions, politics, past and present relationships, spirituality) connects to everything else.

Nevertheless, as both Vaillant (2008) and Campbell (1991) wisely note, such positive emotions or spiritual feelings cannot be expressed adequately in categories or words. Human nature is ambiguous, and so the highest level of scholarship involves paradox not easily articulated. Words limit that part of ourselves that is unlimited. Artists of all stripes best express phenomena or feelings beyond words. Alas, I have looked but cannot find poetry, literature, or scripture (words expressing phenomena beyond words) to express adequately what I am trying to communicate. The quotes beginning this chapter suggest a direction, but it is left to each one of you, dear readers, through your own experiences, relationships, and spiritual journey to find your own way, your own voice, the truth.

As Cari, one of the scholarship students, suggests, "our journey never ends." The El Salvador stories presented in this book will continue to unfold and be told anew for decades to come. James Baldwin (1957/2007), in his short story, *Sonny's Blues*, well describes the telling of the story or journey as follows:

> The blues . . . were not about anything very new. He and his boys up there were keeping it new, at the risk of ruin, destruction, madness and death, in order to find new ways to make us listen. For, while the tale of how we suffer, and how we are delighted, and how we may triumph is never new, it always must be heard. There isn't any other tale to tell, it's the only light we've got in all this darkness.

# REQUEST FOR DONATIONS

........................................................................

We hope to continue to fund the scholarship program in El Salvador to make educational opportunities available to adolescents and young adults who cannot afford an education; to strengthen the screening and mentoring processes; and to pass on leadership and fundraising roles to new generations of like-minded friends behind us. For those interested in supporting deserving students in El Salvador, many of whom this book describes, please consider donations to the following:

        Project Salvador Scholarship Program
        PO Box 300105
        Denver, Colorado 80203
        (Tax ID: 84-1207953)

# ACKNOWLEDGEMENTS

Thanks to my copyeditor, Caitlyn D'Aunno, and my format editor, Ellen C. Maze Sallas, for their good work. Thanks to the El Salvador scholarship students for their permission to publish their statements and their photos. Thanks to my friends for their consultation or comments on the early drafts of this book, including John Kukankos, Julie Spielberger, Karen Rieter, Mike and Susie Jenkins, Marlene Rivera, Karen Scholl, Edwin McCullough, Katelyn Jones, Janna Henning, Tony Gasbarro, Maria Soldad Rivera Bahana, Mary Frances Schneider, and Gene Combs. While I appreciate consultations and support, responsibility for any limitations in the book belongs to me.

Thanks to other friends and colleagues for support through the years, including Victoria Priola Surowiec, Wayne Miller, Don Smith, Mark Stone, Piyush Singh, Joanne Marengo, Fred Hanna, Cristina Cox, Vida Dyson, Christina Jackson, Theresa Fletcher, Josefina Alvarez, Cathy McNeilly, Bill Spielberger, Marty Harrow, Tammy Moore, Maria Schultz, Fatima and Humberto Rivera and their family; my students, friends, and colleagues in the Adler University community; and my family; my parents, Joseph and Irene McDonough Westermeyer, my sister, Mary Jean Rayburn, and my brothers Joseph, Bill, and Mike Westermeyer. Thanks also to Adler University President Ray Crossman, Vice President for Academic Affairs Wendy Paskiewicz, and the Adler University administration for their support over many years.

# REFERENCES

Baldwin, J. (1957/2007). *Sonny's blues.* In Joyce Carol Oates (Ed.), *The oxford book of American short stories.* New York, NY: Oxford University Press.

Banerjee, A. V., & Duflo, E. (2019). *Good economics for hard times.* New York, NY: PublicAffairs.

Brown, L. S. (2008). *Cultural competence in trauma therapy: Beyond the flashback.* Washington, DC: American Psychological Association.

Bukele, N. (interviewee). (December 15, 2019). "Our whole economy is in shatters": President Bukele on the problems facing his country. 60 Minutes Interview.

Byron, Lord G. G., (1992). "She Walks in Beauty." In L. Untermeyer (Comp.), *A Treasury of Great Poems.* New York, NY: Galahad Books.

Campbell, J. (1991). *The power of myth with Bill Moyers.* (Edited by Betty Sue Flowers). New York, NY: Anchor Books.

Combs, G. (2018). White privilege: What's a family therapist to do? *Journal of Marital and Family Therapy, 45*(1), 1–15.

Corrigan, P. W., Druss, B. G., & Perlick, D. A. (2014). The impact of mental illness stigma on seeking and participating in mental health care. *Psychological Science in the Public Interest, 15*(2), 37–70.

Easwaran, E. (1978). *Gandhi the man.* Petaluma, CA: Nilgiri Press.

Erikson, E. H. (1950/1963). *Childhood and society (2nd ed.)*. New York, NY: W.W. Norton & Co.

Frazier, J. B. (2012). *El Salvador could be like that: A memoir of war, politics, and journalism from the front row of the last bloody conflict of the U.S.-Soviet cold war*. Ojai, CA: Karina Library Press.

Freire, P. (1970/2018). *Pedagogy of the oppressed*. New York, NY: Bloomsbury Academic.

Fukuyama, F. (1992/2006). *The end of history and the last man*. New York, NY: Free Press.

Fukuyama, F. (2011). *The origins of political order*. New York, NY: Farrar, Straus & Giroux.

Gandhi, M. K. (1957). *An autobiography: My story of my experiments with truth*. Boston, MA: Beacon Press.

Gates, M. (2019). *The moment of lift: How empowering women changes the world*. New York, NY: Flatiron Books.

Gottesman, I. I. (1991). *Schizophrenia genesis: The origins of madness*. New York, NY: W.W. Freeman and Company.

Gottesman, I. I., & Gould, T. D. (2003). The endophenotype concept in psychiatry: Etymology and strategic intentions. *American Journal of Psychiatry, 160*(4): 636–645.

Herman, J. (1997/2015). *Trauma and recovery*. New York: Basic Books.

Hyde, J. S. (2005). The gender similarities hypothesis. *American Psychologist, 60*(6), 581–592.

Landes, D. S. (1998). *The wealth and poverty of nations: Why some are so rich and some are so poor*. New York, NY: W.W. Norton & Company.

LeVine, R. A., & LeVine, S. (2016). *Do parents matter? Why Japanese sleep soundly, Mexican siblings don't fight, and American families should just relax*. New York, NY: Public Affairs.

LeVine, R. A., LeVine, S., Schnell-Anzola, B., Rowe, J. L., & Dexter, E. (2012). *Literacy and mothering: How women's schooling changes the lives of the world's children*. New York, NY: Oxford University Press, Inc.

LeVine, R. A., & New, R. S. (2008). Introduction. In R. A. LeVine & R. S. New (Eds.), *Anthropology and child development: A cross-cultural reader*. Malden, MA: Blackwell Publishing.

Lobo-Guerrero, C. (2017, November 13). In El Salvador, 'Girls are a problem.' *The New York Times*.

Maddison, M. (2007). *The contours of the world economy 1 – 2030 A.D.: Essays in macro-economic history*. New York, NY: Oxford University Press.

Maimonides, M. (2006). Selection from the Mishneh Torah. In A. David & E. Lynn (Eds), *The civically engaged reader: A diverse collection of short provocative readings on civic activity* (pp. 218–219). Chicago, IL: The Great Books Foundation.

Malkin, E. (2015, September 21). At Salvadoran factory, helping troubled youth makes business sense. *The New York Times.*

Martinez, O., Lemus, E., Martinez, C., & Sontag, D. (2016, November 28). Killers on a shoestring: Inside the gangs of El Salvador. *The New York Times.*

Marquez, G. García. (1982). *Chronicle of a death foretold.* New York, NY: Vintage International.

Moodie, E. (2010). *El Salvador in the aftermath of peace: Crime, uncertainty, and the transition to democracy.* Philadelphia, PA: University of Pennsylvania Press.

Morrison, T. (1970/2007). *The bluest eye.* New York, NY: Vintage International.

O'Leary, B. (1980). An approach to Gandhian economics. *Gandhi Marg, II*(3), 132–147.

Ortiz, M. E. (2017). *My uphill battle: From the streets of L.A. to the streets of El Salvador, the gang enigma never ends.* Lexington, KY: Marvin Edgardo Ortiz.

Perry, B. (2008). Child maltreatment: A neurodevelopmental perspective on the role of trauma and neglect in psychopathology. In T. Beachaine & S. Hinshaw (Eds.), *Child and adolescent psychopathology* (pp. 93–128). New York, NY: John Wiley & Sons.

Pinker, S. (2011). *The better angels of our nature: Why violence has declined.* New York, NY: Penguin.

Pinker, S. (2018). *Enlightenment now: The case for reason, science, humanism, and progress.* New York, NY: Penguin.

Reich, D. (2018). *Who we are and how we got here: Ancient DNA and the new science of the human past*. New York, NY: Pantheon Books.

Ritsner, M. S., & Gottesman, I. I. (2011). The schizophrenia construct after 100 years of challenges. In M. S. Ritsler (Ed.), *Handbook of schizophrenia spectrum disorders, Volume 1 (pp. 1–44)*. New York: Springer Netherlands.

Romero, Óscar. (2018). *The scandal of redemption: When God liberates the poor, saves sinners, and heals nations* (Carolyn Kurtz, Ed.). Walden, NY: Plough Publishing House.

Sachs, J. D. (2005). *The end of poverty: Economic possibilities for our time*. New York, NY: Penguin.

Sachs, J. D. (2015). *The age of sustainable development*. New York, NY: Columbia University Press.

Seeke, C. R. (2017). El Salvador: Background and U.S. relations. Congressional Research Service.

Semple, K. (2019a, June 28). 'I didn't want them to go': Salvadoran family grieves for father and daughter who drowned. *The New York Times*.

Semple, K. (2019b, July 1). 'It is our fault': El Salvador's President takes blame for migrant deaths in Rio Grande. *The New York Times*.

Shaw, G. B., (1921). *Back to Methuselah*, act 1. London: Constable.

Tolstoy, L. (1859/1960). *Death of Ivan Ilyich and other stories*. New York, NY: Signet Classic.

Vaillant, G. E. (1992). The clinical management of immature defenses in the treatment of individuals with personality disorders. In G. E. Vaillant (Ed.), *Ego mechanisms of defense*. Washington, DC: American Psychological Association.

Vaillant, G. E. (1993), *The wisdom of the ego*. Cambridge, MA: Harvard University Press.

Vaillant, G. E. (2002). *Aging Well*. Cambridge, MA: Harvard University Press.

Vaillant, G. E. (2008). *Spiritual evolution*. Cambridge, MA: Broadway Books.

Vaillant, G. E. (2012). *Triumphs of experience*. Cambridge, MA: The Belknap Press of Harvard University Press.

Yunus, M. (2003). *Banker to the poor: Micro-lending and the battle against world poverty*. New York, NY: Public Affairs.

Voisin, D. R. (2019). *American the beautiful and violent: Black youth & neighborhood trauma in Chicago*. New York, NY: Columbia University Press.

Westermeyer, J. F. (1993). Schizophrenia. In P. Tolan and B. Cohler (Eds.), *Handbook of Clinical Research and Practice with Adolescents* (pp. 359–385). New York, NY: John Wiley & Sons.

Westermeyer, J. F. (1998). Predictors and characteristics of mental health among men at midlife: A 32–year longitudinal study. *American Journal of*

*Orthopsychiatry, 68*(2), 265–273.
https://doi.org/10.1037/h0080335

Westermeyer, J. F. (2004). Predictors and characteristics of Erikson's life cycle model among men: A 32-year longitudinal study. *International Journal of Aging and Human Development, 56*(1), 29–48. https://doi.org/10.2190/3VRW-6YP5-PX9T-H0UH

Westermeyer, J. F. (2013). Predictors and characteristics of successful aging among men: A 48-year longitudinal study. *International Journal of Aging and Human Development, 76*(4), 323–345. http://doi.org/10.2190/AG.76.4.c

Westermeyer, J. F., & Harrow, M. (1986). Predicting outcome in schizophrenics and nonschizophrenics of both sexes: The Zigler-Phillips social competence scale. *Journal of Abnormal Psychology, 95*(4), 406–409. https://doi.org/10.1037/0021-843X.95.4.406

Westermeyer, J. F., & Harrow, M. (1988). Course and outcome in schizophrenia. In M. Tsuang & J. C. Simpson (Eds.), *Handbook of Schizophrenia, Volume 3, Nosology, Epidemiology and Genetics* (pp. 205–244). Amsterdam, The Netherlands: Elsevier Science Publishers.

Westermeyer, J. F., Harrow, M., & Marengo, J. T. (1991). Risk for suicide in schizophrenia and other psychotic and nonpsychotic disorders. *Journal of Nervous and Mental Disease, 179*(5), 259–266.

https://doi.org/10.1097/00005053-199105000-00003

Wolfe, S. (2011). Street gangs of El Salvador. In T. Bruneau, L. Dammert, & E. Skinner (Eds.), *Maras: Gang Violence and Security in Central America*. Austin, TX: University of Texas Press.

Wolfe, S. (2017). *Mano dura: The politics of gang control in El Salvador*. Austin, TX: University of Texas Press.

World Bank Group. (2018). *Atlas of sustainable development goals 2018: From world development indicators*. Washington, DC: International Bank for Reconstruction and Development.

# PHOTO ALBUM

1. Cover photo: University scholarship students.

2. Painting of Saint Romero with quote on side of house in El Salvador. (Ch 1)

3. John (left), Jerry (center) with Humberto (right) and Fatima Rivera.

4. Fatima Rivera (left) and John (right) with several high school scholarship students in 2007.

5. Sara as a 14-year-old high school student in 2005. (Ch 3)

6. Dr. Sara as a 27-year-old medical doctor. (Ch 3)

7. Beto, John, and Jerry (back row) and Sara (far right) visiting high school scholarship students.

8. Anna (center) at about age 10 with her two sisters and Mike Jenkins in front of their home. (Ch 4)

9. Anna (left) at age 20 as a nursing student with her mother. (Ch 4) Anna disappeared and is presumed to have been murdered.

10. A monthly gathering of high school and university scholarship students with John, Jerry, and staff.

11. Part of the in-country staff, Tomas (left), Marisol, Anna Valencia, Carmen, and Beto at a monthly meeting where students are mentored.

12. Marisol (left) advising a student.

13. Jasmine with her son, Carlos, shortly before her death of cancer in a hospice. (Ch 6)

14. Jorge with his sister, Erika. (Ch 7)

15. Jorge (center) with his family, John, and Jerry to celebrate his graduation. (Ch 7)

16. Susan, an attorney & vice mayor of her town who graduated several years ago with her brother, Daniel (left). (Ch 9)

17. Children in 2004 returning home with a load of laundry. Children in developing countries often work on household tasks and young children may be responsible for the care of even younger children (see LeVine & LeVine, 2016).

18. Women at a meeting of a microlending organization. (Ch 16)

19. Tony Gasbarro, founder of the Project Salvador Scholarship Program and retired University of Alaska professor.

20. Mike Jenkins, John, and Jerry.

Project Salvador Scholarship Program | PO Box 300105
Denver, Colorado 80203 | (Tax ID: 84-1207953)

Made in the USA
Columbia, SC
23 May 2020